Telecom Providers
Complete Self-Assessment Guide

The guidance in this Self-Assessment is based on Telecom Providers best practices and standards in business process architecture, design and quality management. The guidance is also based on the professional judgment of the individual collaborators listed in the Acknowledgments.

Notice of rights

The information in this book is distributed on an "As Is" basis without warranty. While every precaution has been taken in the preparation of he book, neither the author nor the publisher shall have any liability to any person or entity with respect to any loss or damage caused or alleged to be caused directly or indirectly by the instructions contained in this book or by the products described in it.

Trademarks

Many of the designations used by manufacturers and sellers to distinguish their products are claimed as trademarks. Where those designations appear in this book, and the publisher was aware of a trademark claim, the designations appear as requested by the owner of the trademark. All other product names and services identified throughout this book are used in editorial fashion only and for the benefit of such companies with no intention of infringement of the trademark. No such use, or the use of any trade name, is intended to convey endorsement or other affiliation with this book.

Table of Contents

About The Art of Service

The Art of Service, Business Process Architects since 2000, is dedicated to helping stakeholders achieve excellence.

Defining, designing, creating, and implementing a process to solve a stakeholders challenge or meet an objective is the most valuable role... In EVERY group, company, organization and department.

Unless you're talking a one-time, single-use project, there should be a process. Whether that process is managed and implemented by humans, AI, or a combination of the two, it needs to be designed by someone with a complex enough perspective to ask the right questions.

Someone capable of asking the right questions and step back and say, 'What are we really trying to accomplish here? And is there a different way to look at it?'

With The Art of Service's Standard Requirements Self-Assessments, we empower people who can do just that — whether their title is marketer, entrepreneur, manager, salesperson, consultant, Business Process Manager, executive assistant, IT Manager, CIO etc... —they are the people who rule the future. They are people who watch the process as it happens, and ask the right questions to make the process work better.

Contact us when you need any support with this Self-Assessment and any help with templates, blue-prints and examples of standard documents you might need:

http://theartofservice.com
service@theartofservice.com

Included Resources - how to access

Included with your purchase of the book is the Telecom

Providers Self-Assessment Spreadsheet Dashboard which contains all questions and Self-Assessment areas and auto-generates insights, graphs, and project RACI planning - all with examples to get you started right away.

How? Simply send an email to
access@theartofservice.com
with this books' title in the subject to get the Telecom Providers Self Assessment Tool right away.

You will receive the following contents with New and Updated specific criteria:

- The latest quick edition of the book in PDF

- The latest complete edition of the book in PDF, which criteria correspond to the criteria in...

- The Self-Assessment Excel Dashboard, and...

- Example pre-filled Self-Assessment Excel Dashboard to get familiar with results generation

- In-depth specific Checklists covering the topic

- Project management checklists and templates to assist with implementation

INCLUDES LIFETIME SELF ASSESSMENT UPDATES

Every self assessment comes with Lifetime Updates and Lifetime Free Updated Books. Lifetime Updates is an industry-first feature which allows you to receive verified self assessment updates, ensuring you always have the most accurate information at your fingertips.

Get it now- you will be glad you did - do it now, before you forget.

Send an email to **access@theartofservice.com** with this books' title in the subject to get the Telecom Providers Self Assessment Tool right away.

Purpose of this Self-Assessment

This Self-Assessment has been developed to improve understanding of the requirements and elements of Telecom Providers, based on best practices and standards in business process architecture, design and quality management.

It is designed to allow for a rapid Self-Assessment to determine how closely existing management practices and procedures correspond to the elements of the Self-Assessment.

The criteria of requirements and elements of Telecom Providers have been rephrased in the format of a Self-Assessment questionnaire, with a seven-criterion scoring system, as explained in this document.

In this format, even with limited background knowledge of Telecom Providers, a manager can quickly review existing operations to determine how they measure up to the standards. This in turn can serve as the starting point of a 'gap analysis' to identify management tools or system elements that might usefully be implemented in the organization to help improve overall performance.

How to use the Self-Assessment

On the following pages are a series of questions to identify to what extent your Telecom Providers initiative is complete in comparison to the requirements set in standards.

To facilitate answering the questions, there is a space in front of each question to enter a score on a scale of '1' to '5'.

1 Strongly Disagree

2 Disagree

3 Neutral

4 Agree

5 Strongly Agree

Read the question and rate it with the following in front of mind:

'In my belief,
the answer to this question is clearly defined'.

There are two ways in which you can choose to interpret this statement;
1. how aware are you that the answer to the question is clearly defined
2. for more in-depth analysis you can choose to gather evidence and confirm the answer to the question. This obviously will take more time, most Self-Assessment users opt for the first way to interpret the question and dig deeper later on based on the outcome of the overall Self-Assessment.

A score of '1' would mean that the answer is not clear at all, where a '5' would mean the answer is crystal clear and defined. Leave emtpy when the question is not applicable or you don't want to answer it, you can skip it without affecting your score. Write your score in the space provided.

After you have responded to all the appropriate statements in each section, compute your average score for that section, using the formula provided, and round to the nearest tenth. Then transfer to the corresponding spoke in the Telecom Providers Scorecard on the second next page of the Self-Assessment.

Your completed Telecom Providers Scorecard will give you a clear presentation of which Telecom Providers areas need attention.

Telecom Providers Scorecard Example

Example of how the finalized Scorecard can look like:

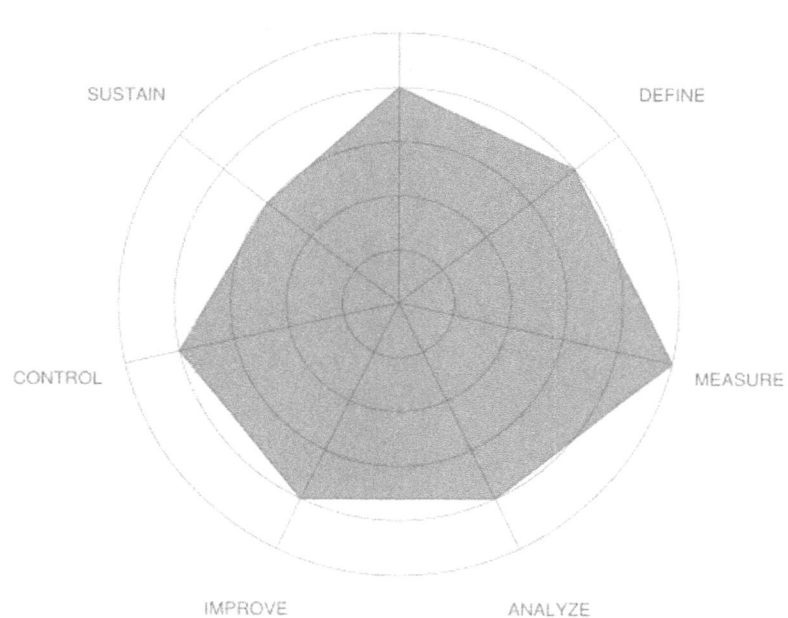

Telecom Providers Scorecard

Your Scores:

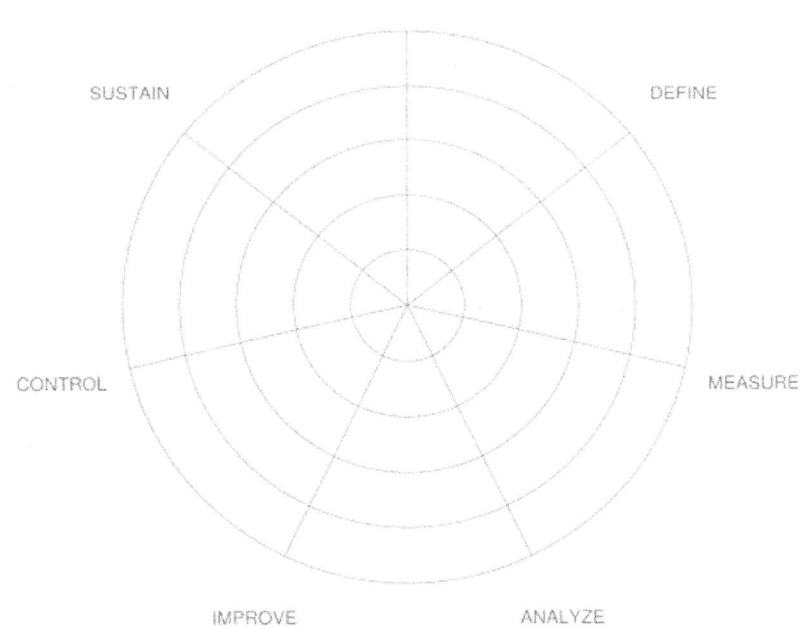

BEGINNING OF THE SELF-ASSESSMENT:

CRITERION #1: RECOGNIZE

INTENT: Be aware of the need for change. Recognize that there is an unfavorable variation, problem or symptom.

In my belief, the answer to this question is clearly defined:

5 Strongly Agree

4 Agree

3 Neutral

2 Disagree

1 Strongly Disagree

1. What telecom providers problem should be solved?
<--- Score

2. Will telecom providers deliverables need to be tested and, if so, by whom?
<--- Score

3. How do you recognize an objection?

<--- Score

4. Are employees recognized for desired behaviors?
<--- Score

5. Will a response program recognize when a crisis occurs and provide some level of response?
<--- Score

6. What are the telecom providers resources needed?
<--- Score

7. What is the extent or complexity of the telecom providers problem?
<--- Score

8. When a telecom providers manager recognizes a problem, what options are available?
<--- Score

9. How much are sponsors, customers, partners, stakeholders involved in telecom providers? In other words, what are the risks, if telecom providers does not deliver successfully?
<--- Score

10. Do you know what you need to know about telecom providers?
<--- Score

11. What training and capacity building actions are needed to implement proposed reforms?
<--- Score

12. How many trainings, in total, are needed?
<--- Score

13. What are the timeframes required to resolve each of the issues/problems?
<--- Score

14. What is the telecom providers problem definition? What do you need to resolve?
<--- Score

15. What information do users need?
<--- Score

16. Are you dealing with any of the same issues today as yesterday? What can you do about this?
<--- Score

17. What telecom providers coordination do you need?
<--- Score

18. What problems are you facing and how do you consider telecom providers will circumvent those obstacles?
<--- Score

19. Which issues are too important to ignore?
<--- Score

20. Will it solve real problems?
<--- Score

21. Are there any revenue recognition issues?
<--- Score

22. How are you going to measure success?
<--- Score

23. Are there regulatory / compliance issues?
<--- Score

24. What prevents you from making the changes you know will make you a more effective telecom providers leader?
<--- Score

25. Who needs to know?
<--- Score

26. What are the clients issues and concerns?
<--- Score

27. Will new equipment/products be required to facilitate telecom providers delivery, for example is new software needed?
<--- Score

28. Do you need different information or graphics?
<--- Score

29. Did you miss any major telecom providers issues?
<--- Score

30. Why the need?
<--- Score

31. What needs to stay?
<--- Score

32. Looking at each person individually – does every one have the qualities which are needed to work in this group?
<--- Score

33. What activities does the governance board need to consider?
<--- Score

34. What else needs to be measured?
<--- Score

35. Is the need for organizational change recognized?
<--- Score

36. What creative shifts do you need to take?
<--- Score

37. What is the problem and/or vulnerability?
<--- Score

38. Consider your own telecom providers project, what types of organizational problems do you think might be causing or affecting your problem, based on the work done so far?
<--- Score

39. What telecom providers capabilities do you need?
<--- Score

40. Who else hopes to benefit from it?
<--- Score

41. What are your needs in relation to telecom providers skills, labor, equipment, and markets?
<--- Score

42. Does the problem have ethical dimensions?
<--- Score

43. What vendors make products that address the telecom providers needs?
<--- Score

44. Which needs are not included or involved?
<--- Score

45. As a sponsor, customer or management, how important is it to meet goals, objectives?
<--- Score

46. Where is training needed?
<--- Score

47. Where do you need to exercise leadership?
<--- Score

48. Does your organization need more telecom providers education?
<--- Score

49. What are the stakeholder objectives to be achieved with telecom providers?
<--- Score

50. Who are your key stakeholders who need to sign off?
<--- Score

51. Who needs to know about telecom providers?
<--- Score

52. What would happen if telecom providers weren't done?
<--- Score

53. To what extent does each concerned units management team recognize telecom providers as an effective investment?
<--- Score

54. How do you assess your telecom providers workforce capability and capacity needs, including skills, competencies, and staffing levels?
<--- Score

55. How can auditing be a preventative security measure?
<--- Score

56. Can management personnel recognize the monetary benefit of telecom providers?
<--- Score

57. How do you identify the kinds of information that you will need?
<--- Score

58. What is the smallest subset of the problem you can usefully solve?
<--- Score

59. Is the quality assurance team identified?
<--- Score

60. What do you need to start doing?
<--- Score

61. Why is this needed?
<--- Score

62. Have you identified your telecom providers key

performance indicators?

<--- Score

63. Who defines the rules in relation to any given issue?

<--- Score

64. Are there recognized telecom providers problems?

<--- Score

65. Who needs budgets?

<--- Score

66. How do you recognize an telecom providers objection?

<--- Score

67. Think about the people you identified for your telecom providers project and the project responsibilities you would assign to them, what kind of training do you think they would need to perform these responsibilities effectively?

<--- Score

68. For your telecom providers project, identify and describe the business environment, is there more than one layer to the business environment?

<--- Score

69. What telecom providers events should you attend?

<--- Score

70. Does telecom providers create potential expectations in other areas that need to be recognized and considered?

<--- Score

71. How do you take a forward-looking perspective in identifying telecom providers research related to market response and models?
<--- Score

72. What are the expected benefits of telecom providers to the stakeholder?
<--- Score

73. Are there any specific expectations or concerns about the telecom providers team, telecom providers itself?
<--- Score

74. What should be considered when identifying available resources, constraints, and deadlines?
<--- Score

75. Do you recognize telecom providers achievements?
<--- Score

76. Is it needed?
<--- Score

77. What do employees need in the short term?
<--- Score

78. Which information does the telecom providers business case need to include?
<--- Score

79. What extra resources will you need?
<--- Score

80. How are the telecom providers's objectives aligned to the group's overall stakeholder strategy?
<--- Score

81. Are there telecom providers problems defined?
<--- Score

82. What tools and technologies are needed for a custom telecom providers project?
<--- Score

83. Are controls defined to recognize and contain problems?
<--- Score

84. Would you recognize a threat from the inside?
<--- Score

85. How are training requirements identified?
<--- Score

86. To what extent would your organization benefit from being recognized as a award recipient?
<--- Score

87. What is the recognized need?
<--- Score

88. What are the minority interests and what amount of minority interests can be recognized?
<--- Score

89. Whom do you really need or want to serve?
<--- Score

90. Are problem definition and motivation clearly presented?

<--- Score

91. What does telecom providers success mean to the stakeholders?

<--- Score

92. What situation(s) led to this telecom providers Self Assessment?

<--- Score

93. Do you need to avoid or amend any telecom providers activities?

<--- Score

94. What needs to be done?

<--- Score

95. Is it clear when you think of the day ahead of you what activities and tasks you need to complete?

<--- Score

96. Do you have/need 24-hour access to key personnel?

<--- Score

97. Are employees recognized or rewarded for performance that demonstrates the highest levels of integrity?

<--- Score

Add up total points for this section:
_ _ _ _ _ = Total points for this section

Divided by: _____ (number of
statements answered) = _____
Average score for this section

Transfer your score to the telecom
providers Index at the beginning of the
Self-Assessment.

CRITERION #2: DEFINE:

INTENT: Formulate the stakeholder problem. Define the problem, needs and objectives.

In my belief, the answer to this question is clearly defined:

5 Strongly Agree

4 Agree

3 Neutral

2 Disagree

1 Strongly Disagree

1. How and when will the baselines be defined?
<--- Score

2. Are roles and responsibilities formally defined?
<--- Score

3. How do you gather telecom providers requirements?
<--- Score

4. What is the definition of telecom providers excellence?
<--- Score

5. How will the telecom providers team and the group measure complete success of telecom providers?
<--- Score

6. Is the work to date meeting requirements?
<--- Score

7. What happens if telecom providers's scope changes?
<--- Score

8. Where can you gather more information?
<--- Score

9. Are resources adequate for the scope?
<--- Score

10. Do the problem and goal statements meet the SMART criteria (specific, measurable, attainable, relevant, and time-bound)?
<--- Score

11. Has a high-level 'as is' process map been completed, verified and validated?
<--- Score

12. Has your scope been defined?
<--- Score

13. What defines best in class?
<--- Score

14. What are the compelling stakeholder reasons for embarking on telecom providers?
<--- Score

15. In what way can you redefine the criteria of choice clients have in your category in your favor?
<--- Score

16. What information should you gather?
<--- Score

17. Are required metrics defined, what are they?
<--- Score

18. Is the scope of telecom providers defined?
<--- Score

19. How do you build the right business case?
<--- Score

20. What is the scope of the telecom providers work?
<--- Score

21. Are the telecom providers requirements testable?
<--- Score

22. How do you hand over telecom providers context?
<--- Score

23. Is special telecom providers user knowledge required?
<--- Score

24. What is the context?

<--- Score

25. Is there any additional telecom providers definition of success?

<--- Score

26. What are the telecom providers tasks and definitions?

<--- Score

27. Is telecom providers required?

<--- Score

28. What are the tasks and definitions?

<--- Score

29. What critical content must be communicated – who, what, when, where, and how?

<--- Score

30. Are there any constraints known that bear on the ability to perform telecom providers work? How is the team addressing them?

<--- Score

31. Will team members perform telecom providers work when assigned and in a timely fashion?

<--- Score

32. What is the scope of telecom providers?

<--- Score

33. What would be the goal or target for a telecom providers's improvement team?

<--- Score

34. Are customer(s) identified and segmented according to their different needs and requirements?
<--- Score

35. Are there different segments of customers?
<--- Score

36. Has the direction changed at all during the course of telecom providers? If so, when did it change and why?
<--- Score

37. When is/was the telecom providers start date?
<--- Score

38. What is in the scope and what is not in scope?
<--- Score

39. Are different versions of process maps needed to account for the different types of inputs?
<--- Score

40. What is the definition of success?
<--- Score

41. What are the boundaries of the scope? What is in bounds and what is not? What is the start point? What is the stop point?
<--- Score

42. Has a project plan, Gantt chart, or similar been developed/completed?
<--- Score

43. Has anyone else (internal or external to the group) attempted to solve this problem or a similar one

before? If so, what knowledge can be leveraged from these previous efforts?

<--- Score

44. Who defines (or who defined) the rules and roles?

<--- Score

45. What are the requirements for audit information?

<--- Score

46. Are accountability and ownership for telecom providers clearly defined?

<--- Score

47. Is telecom providers linked to key stakeholder goals and objectives?

<--- Score

48. If substitutes have been appointed, have they been briefed on the telecom providers goals and received regular communications as to the progress to date?

<--- Score

49. Are approval levels defined for contracts and supplements to contracts?

<--- Score

50. What was the context?

<--- Score

51. Who is gathering information?

<--- Score

52. Will team members regularly document their

telecom providers work?
<--- Score

53. Do you all define telecom providers in the same way?
<--- Score

54. How will variation in the actual durations of each activity be dealt with to ensure that the expected telecom providers results are met?
<--- Score

55. What is out-of-scope initially?
<--- Score

56. Are improvement team members fully trained on telecom providers?
<--- Score

57. What scope to assess?
<--- Score

58. What is a worst-case scenario for losses?
<--- Score

59. Is telecom providers currently on schedule according to the plan?
<--- Score

60. How have you defined all telecom providers requirements first?
<--- Score

61. What knowledge or experience is required?
<--- Score

62. How do you manage scope?
<--- Score

63. Have all basic functions of telecom providers been defined?
<--- Score

64. How is the team tracking and documenting its work?
<--- Score

65. Has a team charter been developed and communicated?
<--- Score

66. Scope of sensitive information?
<--- Score

67. Are the telecom providers requirements complete?
<--- Score

68. What sources do you use to gather information for a telecom providers study?
<--- Score

69. Is there a telecom providers management charter, including stakeholder case, problem and goal statements, scope, milestones, roles and responsibilities, communication plan?
<--- Score

70. Do you have a telecom providers success story or case study ready to tell and share?
<--- Score

71. Have specific policy objectives been defined?
<--- Score

72. What intelligence can you gather?
<--- Score

73. What scope do you want your strategy to cover?
<--- Score

74. Who approved the telecom providers scope?
<--- Score

75. What key stakeholder process output measure(s) does telecom providers leverage and how?
<--- Score

76. What are the rough order estimates on cost savings/opportunities that telecom providers brings?
<--- Score

77. How would you define telecom providers leadership?
<--- Score

78. Is the telecom providers scope complete and appropriately sized?
<--- Score

79. What customer feedback methods were used to solicit their input?
<--- Score

80. What are (control) requirements for telecom providers Information?
<--- Score

81. Who is gathering telecom providers information?
<--- Score

82. How often are the team meetings?
<--- Score

83. How do you manage unclear telecom providers requirements?
<--- Score

84. Has everyone on the team, including the team leaders, been properly trained?
<--- Score

85. Is there a completed, verified, and validated high-level 'as is' (not 'should be' or 'could be') stakeholder process map?
<--- Score

86. Does the scope remain the same?
<--- Score

87. How do you keep key subject matter experts in the loop?
<--- Score

88. What specifically is the problem? Where does it occur? When does it occur? What is its extent?
<--- Score

89. Is there regularly 100% attendance at the team meetings? If not, have appointed substitutes attended to preserve cross-functionality and full representation?
<--- Score

90. When are meeting minutes sent out? Who is on the distribution list?

<--- Score

91. Have the customer needs been translated into specific, measurable requirements? How?

<--- Score

92. How was the 'as is' process map developed, reviewed, verified and validated?

<--- Score

93. Is there a critical path to deliver telecom providers results?

<--- Score

94. What gets examined?

<--- Score

95. Has the telecom providers work been fairly and/or equitably divided and delegated among team members who are qualified and capable to perform the work? Has everyone contributed?

<--- Score

96. Are all requirements met?

<--- Score

97. What telecom providers requirements should be gathered?

<--- Score

98. Is full participation by members in regularly held team meetings guaranteed?

<--- Score

99. What is in scope?
<--- Score

100. How would you define the culture at your organization, how susceptible is it to telecom providers changes?
<--- Score

101. What baselines are required to be defined and managed?
<--- Score

102. What constraints exist that might impact the team?
<--- Score

103. Has the improvement team collected the 'voice of the customer' (obtained feedback – qualitative and quantitative)?
<--- Score

104. Is the current 'as is' process being followed? If not, what are the discrepancies?
<--- Score

105. What is the scope?
<--- Score

106. How can the value of telecom providers be defined?
<--- Score

107. What is the worst case scenario?
<--- Score

108. What are the dynamics of the communication plan?
<--- Score

109. Why are you doing telecom providers and what is the scope?
<--- Score

110. Is the team adequately staffed with the desired cross-functionality? If not, what additional resources are available to the team?
<--- Score

111. How does the telecom providers manager ensure against scope creep?
<--- Score

112. How are consistent telecom providers definitions important?
<--- Score

113. Is it clearly defined in and to your organization what you do?
<--- Score

114. Who are the telecom providers improvement team members, including Management Leads and Coaches?
<--- Score

115. When is the estimated completion date?
<--- Score

116. What is out of scope?
<--- Score

117. How did the telecom providers manager receive input to the development of a telecom providers improvement plan and the estimated completion dates/times of each activity?
<--- Score

118. Is the team equipped with available and reliable resources?
<--- Score

119. Is data collected and displayed to better understand customer(s) critical needs and requirements.
<--- Score

120. What are the core elements of the telecom providers business case?
<--- Score

121. What is the scope of the telecom providers effort?
<--- Score

122. Is the telecom providers scope manageable?
<--- Score

123. What sort of initial information to gather?
<--- Score

124. Will a telecom providers production readiness review be required?
<--- Score

125. Does the team have regular meetings?
<--- Score

126. Are audit criteria, scope, frequency and methods defined?

<--- Score

127. What system do you use for gathering telecom providers information?

<--- Score

128. How do you gather the stories?

<--- Score

129. How do you catch telecom providers definition inconsistencies?

<--- Score

130. Is there a completed SIPOC representation, describing the Suppliers, Inputs, Process, Outputs, and Customers?

<--- Score

131. Have all of the relationships been defined properly?

<--- Score

132. Is there a clear telecom providers case definition?

<--- Score

133. Do you have organizational privacy requirements?

<--- Score

134. What are the Roles and Responsibilities for each team member and its leadership? Where is this documented?

<--- Score

135. Is scope creep really all bad news?
<--- Score

136. Is the improvement team aware of the different versions of a process: what they think it is vs. what it actually is vs. what it should be vs. what it could be?
<--- Score

137. Has/have the customer(s) been identified?
<--- Score

138. What telecom providers services do you require?
<--- Score

139. How do you manage changes in telecom providers requirements?
<--- Score

140. What are the telecom providers use cases?
<--- Score

141. The political context: who holds power?
<--- Score

Add up total points for this section:
_ _ _ _ _   = Total points for this section

Divided by: _ _ _ _ _ _ (number of statements answered) = _ _ _ _ _ _
Average score for this section

Transfer your score to the telecom providers Index at the beginning of the Self-Assessment.

CRITERION #3: MEASURE:

INTENT: Gather the correct data.
Measure the current performance and
evolution of the situation.

In my belief, the answer to this
question is clearly defined:

5 Strongly Agree

4 Agree

3 Neutral

2 Disagree

1 Strongly Disagree

1. Does a telecom providers quantification method exist?
<--- Score

2. How will effects be measured?
<--- Score

3. How is progress measured?
<--- Score

4. What disadvantage does this cause for the user?
<--- Score

5. Where can you go to verify the info?
<--- Score

6. What details are required of the telecom providers cost structure?
<--- Score

7. How will you measure success?
<--- Score

8. How do you measure efficient delivery of telecom providers services?
<--- Score

9. What causes innovation to fail or succeed in your organization?
<--- Score

10. What do you measure and why?
<--- Score

11. Are telecom providers vulnerabilities categorized and prioritized?
<--- Score

12. Where is the cost?
<--- Score

13. Who should receive measurement reports?
<--- Score

14. What does your operating model cost?

<--- Score

15. Which measures and indicators matter?
<--- Score

16. What are the telecom providers key cost drivers?
<--- Score

17. What would be a real cause for concern?
<--- Score

18. What is the total fixed cost?
<--- Score

19. What are the current costs of the telecom providers process?
<--- Score

20. What is the root cause(s) of the problem?
<--- Score

21. Has a cost center been established?
<--- Score

22. What causes extra work or rework?
<--- Score

23. How do you measure lifecycle phases?
<--- Score

24. How can you manage cost down?
<--- Score

25. What would it cost to replace your technology?
<--- Score

26. What harm might be caused?
<--- Score

27. Are the telecom providers benefits worth its costs?
<--- Score

28. What evidence is there and what is measured?
<--- Score

29. Are there measurements based on task performance?
<--- Score

30. How can you reduce the costs of obtaining inputs?
<--- Score

31. What tests verify requirements?
<--- Score

32. How do you quantify and qualify impacts?
<--- Score

33. How do you aggregate measures across priorities?
<--- Score

34. How will your organization measure success?
<--- Score

35. What does losing customers cost your organization?
<--- Score

36. How do you verify and validate the telecom providers data?
<--- Score

37. How do you control the overall costs of your work processes?
<--- Score

38. Have design-to-cost goals been established?
<--- Score

39. What are the operational costs after telecom providers deployment?
<--- Score

40. Are you able to realize any cost savings?
<--- Score

41. How to cause the change?
<--- Score

42. Are supply costs steady or fluctuating?
<--- Score

43. What are the uncertainties surrounding estimates of impact?
<--- Score

44. How frequently do you verify your telecom providers strategy?
<--- Score

45. How do you verify the authenticity of the data and information used?
<--- Score

46. Who is involved in verifying compliance?
<--- Score

47. At what cost?
<--- Score

48. Are indirect costs charged to the telecom providers program?
<--- Score

49. What measurements are being captured?
<--- Score

50. Is there an opportunity to verify requirements?
<--- Score

51. How do your measurements capture actionable telecom providers information for use in exceeding your customers expectations and securing your customers engagement?
<--- Score

52. What are the costs of delaying telecom providers action?
<--- Score

53. Was a business case (cost/benefit) developed?
<--- Score

54. What is your telecom providers quality cost segregation study?
<--- Score

55. What are allowable costs?
<--- Score

56. What are the costs and benefits?
<--- Score

57. Do you effectively measure and reward individual and team performance?
<--- Score

58. Are you aware of what could cause a problem?
<--- Score

59. How long to keep data and how to manage retention costs?
<--- Score

60. Do you have a flow diagram of what happens?
<--- Score

61. Are there competing telecom providers priorities?
<--- Score

62. Does the telecom providers task fit the client's priorities?
<--- Score

63. What do people want to verify?
<--- Score

64. How do you verify performance?
<--- Score

65. What are your primary costs, revenues, assets?
<--- Score

66. Which telecom providers impacts are significant?
<--- Score

67. What can be used to verify compliance?
<--- Score

68. What are the costs?
<--- Score

69. How are measurements made?
<--- Score

70. When should you bother with diagrams?
<--- Score

71. What could cause you to change course?
<--- Score

72. Are actual costs in line with budgeted costs?
<--- Score

73. What is the cost of rework?
<--- Score

74. What measurements are possible, practicable and meaningful?
<--- Score

75. What are your customers expectations and measures?
<--- Score

76. How do you verify and develop ideas and innovations?
<--- Score

77. Which costs should be taken into account?
<--- Score

78. How will measures be used to manage and adapt?
<--- Score

79. What are the telecom providers investment costs?
<--- Score

80. What is your decision requirements diagram?
<--- Score

81. Is it possible to estimate the impact of unanticipated complexity such as wrong or failed assumptions, feedback, etcetera on proposed reforms?
<--- Score

82. How can you measure the performance?
<--- Score

83. What is an unallowable cost?
<--- Score

84. Are there any easy-to-implement alternatives to telecom providers? Sometimes other solutions are available that do not require the cost implications of a full-blown project?
<--- Score

85. How do you prevent mis-estimating cost?
<--- Score

86. How do you verify telecom providers completeness and accuracy?
<--- Score

87. When are costs are incurred?
<--- Score

88. Is the cost worth the telecom providers effort ?
<--- Score

89. Are the measurements objective?

<--- Score

90. How will costs be allocated?

<--- Score

91. Do the benefits outweigh the costs?

<--- Score

92. What potential environmental factors impact the telecom providers effort?

<--- Score

93. What are hidden telecom providers quality costs?

<--- Score

94. What relevant entities could be measured?

<--- Score

95. What are the costs of reform?

<--- Score

96. What are the strategic priorities for this year?

<--- Score

97. Is the solution cost-effective?

<--- Score

98. How is performance measured?

<--- Score

99. Does management have the right priorities among projects?

<--- Score

100. How can a telecom providers test verify your ideas or assumptions?
<--- Score

101. What users will be impacted?
<--- Score

102. How will you measure your telecom providers effectiveness?
<--- Score

103. Have you included everything in your telecom providers cost models?
<--- Score

104. What happens if cost savings do not materialize?
<--- Score

105. How do you measure variability?
<--- Score

106. What is measured? Why?
<--- Score

107. How sensitive must the telecom providers strategy be to cost?
<--- Score

108. What are you verifying?
<--- Score

109. Are you taking your company in the direction of better and revenue or cheaper and cost?
<--- Score

110. Who pays the cost?
<--- Score

111. Do you have an issue in getting priority?
<--- Score

112. Where is it measured?
<--- Score

113. How can you measure telecom providers in a systematic way?
<--- Score

114. What is the telecom providers business impact?
<--- Score

115. How do you verify the telecom providers requirements quality?
<--- Score

116. How do you verify your resources?
<--- Score

117. How frequently do you track telecom providers measures?
<--- Score

118. How much does it cost?
<--- Score

119. Why do you expend time and effort to implement measurement, for whom?
<--- Score

120. Why do the measurements/indicators matter?
<--- Score

121. How are you verifying it?
<--- Score

122. What is the cause of any telecom providers gaps?
<--- Score

123. How are costs allocated?
<--- Score

124. Do you verify that corrective actions were taken?
<--- Score

125. When a disaster occurs, who gets priority?
<--- Score

126. Do you aggressively reward and promote the people who have the biggest impact on creating excellent telecom providers services/products?
<--- Score

127. What could cause delays in the schedule?
<--- Score

128. What causes investor action?
<--- Score

129. What drives O&M cost?
<--- Score

130. What are the types and number of measures to use?
<--- Score

131. Have you made assumptions about the shape of

the future, particularly its impact on your customers and competitors?
<--- Score

132. What causes mismanagement?
<--- Score

133. Did you tackle the cause or the symptom?
<--- Score

134. What methods are feasible and acceptable to estimate the impact of reforms?
<--- Score

Add up total points for this section:
_____ = Total points for this section

Divided by: _____ (number of statements answered) = _____
Average score for this section

Transfer your score to the telecom providers Index at the beginning of the Self-Assessment.

CRITERION #4: ANALYZE:

INTENT: Analyze causes, assumptions
and hypotheses.

In my belief, the answer to this
question is clearly defined:

5 Strongly Agree

4 Agree

3 Neutral

2 Disagree

1 Strongly Disagree

1. Is the final output clearly identified?
<--- Score

2. What conclusions were drawn from the team's data
collection and analysis? How did the team reach these
conclusions?
<--- Score

3. Is data and process analysis, root cause analysis and
quantifying the gap/opportunity in place?

<--- Score

4. Do quality systems drive continuous improvement?
<--- Score

5. Have any additional benefits been identified that will result from closing all or most of the gaps?
<--- Score

6. Are all team members qualified for all tasks?
<--- Score

7. Do you have the authority to produce the output?
<--- Score

8. How do mission and objectives affect the telecom providers processes of your organization?
<--- Score

9. What internal processes need improvement?
<--- Score

10. Has data output been validated?
<--- Score

11. Was a cause-and-effect diagram used to explore the different types of causes (or sources of variation)?
<--- Score

12. How do you define collaboration and team output?
<--- Score

13. What qualifications do telecom providers leaders need?
<--- Score

14. What qualifications are necessary?
<--- Score

15. Who will gather what data?
<--- Score

16. Are all staff in core telecom providers subjects Highly Qualified?
<--- Score

17. Is the suppliers process defined and controlled?
<--- Score

18. Do your employees have the opportunity to do what they do best everyday?
<--- Score

19. What qualifications are needed?
<--- Score

20. What resources go in to get the desired output?
<--- Score

21. Are telecom providers changes recognized early enough to be approved through the regular process?
<--- Score

22. What are your current levels and trends in key measures or indicators of telecom providers product and process performance that are important to and directly serve your customers? How do these results compare with the performance of your competitors and other organizations with similar offerings?

<--- Score

23. How is the telecom providers Value Stream Mapping managed?
<--- Score

24. Do several people in different organizational units assist with the telecom providers process?
<--- Score

25. What process improvements will be needed?
<--- Score

26. How much data can be collected in the given timeframe?
<--- Score

27. Identify an operational issue in your organization, for example, could a particular task be done more quickly or more efficiently by telecom providers?
<--- Score

28. What controls do you have in place to protect data?
<--- Score

29. How can risk management be tied procedurally to process elements?
<--- Score

30. An organizationally feasible system request is one that considers the mission, goals and objectives of the organization, key questions are: is the telecom providers solution request practical and will it solve a problem or take advantage of an opportunity to achieve company goals?

<--- Score

31. What output to create?
<--- Score

32. What is the complexity of the output produced?
<--- Score

33. How do you use telecom providers data and information to support organizational decision making and innovation?
<--- Score

34. What telecom providers data will be collected?
<--- Score

35. What quality tools were used to get through the analyze phase?
<--- Score

36. Who gets your output?
<--- Score

37. A compounding model resolution with available relevant data can often provide insight towards a solution methodology; which telecom providers models, tools and techniques are necessary?
<--- Score

38. What is your organizations system for selecting qualified vendors?
<--- Score

39. Do staff qualifications match your project?
<--- Score

40. How was the detailed process map generated, verified, and validated?
<--- Score

41. What tools were used to generate the list of possible causes?
<--- Score

42. Is the required telecom providers data gathered?
<--- Score

43. What qualifications and skills do you need?
<--- Score

44. Has an output goal been set?
<--- Score

45. What are the telecom providers design outputs?
<--- Score

46. What tools were used to narrow the list of possible causes?
<--- Score

47. Think about some of the processes you undertake within your organization, which do you own?
<--- Score

48. Do you understand your management processes today?
<--- Score

49. What were the financial benefits resulting from any 'ground fruit or low-hanging fruit' (quick fixes)?
<--- Score

50. Is pre-qualification of suppliers carried out?
<--- Score

51. What is the output?
<--- Score

52. Who will facilitate the team and process?
<--- Score

53. Is the performance gap determined?
<--- Score

54. Who is involved in the management review
process?
<--- Score

55. Have the problem and goal statements been
updated to reflect the additional knowledge gained
from the analyze phase?
<--- Score

56. How is the way you as the leader think and process
information affecting your organizational culture?
<--- Score

57. Who is involved with workflow mapping?
<--- Score

**58. What are your key performance measures or
indicators and in-process measures for the control
and improvement of your telecom providers
processes?**
<--- Score

59. Is there any way to speed up the process?

<--- Score

60. Were there any improvement opportunities identified from the process analysis?
<--- Score

61. What are the best opportunities for value improvement?
<--- Score

62. What does the data say about the performance of the stakeholder process?
<--- Score

63. What telecom providers data should be managed?
<--- Score

64. How is the data gathered?
<--- Score

65. What successful thing are you doing today that may be blinding you to new growth opportunities?
<--- Score

66. How do you measure the operational performance of your key work systems and processes, including productivity, cycle time, and other appropriate measures of process effectiveness, efficiency, and innovation?
<--- Score

67. Who owns what data?
<--- Score

68. How often will data be collected for measures?
<--- Score

69. Is the telecom providers process severely broken such that a re-design is necessary?
<--- Score

70. How are outputs preserved and protected?
<--- Score

71. How does the organization define, manage, and improve its telecom providers processes?
<--- Score

72. What did the team gain from developing a sub-process map?
<--- Score

73. What are the disruptive telecom providers technologies that enable your organization to radically change your business processes?
<--- Score

74. Where is the data coming from to measure compliance?
<--- Score

75. What are the processes for audit reporting and management?
<--- Score

76. Is there an established change management process?
<--- Score

77. How do you identify specific telecom providers investment opportunities and emerging trends?
<--- Score

78. What are the telecom providers business drivers?
<--- Score

79. What are evaluation criteria for the output?
<--- Score

80. What are your best practices for minimizing telecom providers project risk, while demonstrating incremental value and quick wins throughout the telecom providers project lifecycle?
<--- Score

81. Where can you get qualified talent today?
<--- Score

82. How is data used for program management and improvement?
<--- Score

83. What training and qualifications will you need?
<--- Score

84. Were Pareto charts (or similar) used to portray the 'heavy hitters' (or key sources of variation)?
<--- Score

85. What do you need to qualify?
<--- Score

86. Were any designed experiments used to generate additional insight into the data analysis?
<--- Score

87. What is the cost of poor quality as supported by

the team's analysis?
<--- Score

88. What are the personnel training and qualifications required?
<--- Score

89. Are your outputs consistent?
<--- Score

90. Have you defined which data is gathered how?
<--- Score

91. How do your work systems and key work processes relate to and capitalize on your core competencies?
<--- Score

92. What will drive telecom providers change?
<--- Score

93. Which telecom providers data should be retained?
<--- Score

94. Is there a strict change management process?
<--- Score

95. What are the revised rough estimates of the financial savings/opportunity for telecom providers improvements?
<--- Score

96. What is your organizations process which leads to recognition of value generation?
<--- Score

97. Where is telecom providers data gathered?
<--- Score

98. How do you promote understanding that opportunity for improvement is not criticism of the status quo, or the people who created the status quo?
<--- Score

99. What telecom providers metrics are outputs of the process?
<--- Score

100. Think about the functions involved in your telecom providers project, what processes flow from these functions?
<--- Score

101. What, related to, telecom providers processes does your organization outsource?
<--- Score

102. What other jobs or tasks affect the performance of the steps in the telecom providers process?
<--- Score

103. How difficult is it to qualify what telecom providers ROI is?
<--- Score

104. What qualifies as competition?
<--- Score

105. What is the oversight process?
<--- Score

106. What types of data do your telecom providers

indicators require?
<--- Score

107. What methods do you use to gather telecom providers data?
<--- Score

108. Who qualifies to gain access to data?
<--- Score

109. What data do you need to collect?
<--- Score

110. Do your contracts/agreements contain data security obligations?
<--- Score

111. What kind of crime could a potential new hire have committed that would not only not disqualify him/her from being hired by your organization, but would actually indicate that he/she might be a particularly good fit?
<--- Score

112. How many input/output points does it require?
<--- Score

113. How will the change process be managed?
<--- Score

114. What are your current levels and trends in key telecom providers measures or indicators of product and process performance that are important to and directly serve your customers?
<--- Score

115. Do you, as a leader, bounce back quickly from setbacks?

<--- Score

116. What are your outputs?

<--- Score

117. What data is gathered?

<--- Score

118. How is telecom providers data gathered?

<--- Score

119. What telecom providers data should be collected?

<--- Score

120. What information qualified as important?

<--- Score

121. What were the crucial 'moments of truth' on the process map?

<--- Score

122. How has the telecom providers data been gathered?

<--- Score

123. What other organizational variables, such as reward systems or communication systems, affect the performance of this telecom providers process?

<--- Score

124. How will the telecom providers data be captured?

<--- Score

125. Do your leaders quickly bounce back from setbacks?
<--- Score

126. What telecom providers data do you gather or use now?
<--- Score

127. How do you ensure that the telecom providers opportunity is realistic?
<--- Score

128. What are your telecom providers processes?
<--- Score

129. Should you invest in industry-recognized qualifications?
<--- Score

130. Was a detailed process map created to amplify critical steps of the 'as is' stakeholder process?
<--- Score

131. How do you implement and manage your work processes to ensure that they meet design requirements?
<--- Score

132. How will the data be checked for quality?
<--- Score

133. What is the telecom providers Driver?
<--- Score

134. Is the gap/opportunity displayed and

communicated in financial terms?
<--- Score

135. Can you add value to the current telecom providers decision-making process (largely qualitative) by incorporating uncertainty modeling (more quantitative)?
<--- Score

Add up total points for this section:
_ _ _ _ _ = Total points for this section

Divided by: _ _ _ _ _ _ (number of statements answered) = _ _ _ _ _ _
Average score for this section

Transfer your score to the telecom providers Index at the beginning of the Self-Assessment.

CRITERION #5: IMPROVE:

INTENT: Develop a practical solution. Innovate, establish and test the solution and to measure the results.

In my belief, the answer to this question is clearly defined:

5 Strongly Agree

4 Agree

3 Neutral

2 Disagree

1 Strongly Disagree

1. Are you assessing telecom providers and risk?
<--- Score

2. Is the telecom providers risk managed?
<--- Score

3. What tools do you use once you have decided on a telecom providers strategy and more importantly how do you choose?

<--- Score

4. Who do you report telecom providers results to?
<--- Score

5. How do you measure progress and evaluate training effectiveness?
<--- Score

6. What is the risk?
<--- Score

7. Is the scope clearly documented?
<--- Score

8. What practices helps your organization to develop its capacity to recognize patterns?
<--- Score

9. How can you improve telecom providers?
<--- Score

10. Are risk triggers captured?
<--- Score

11. How do the telecom providers results compare with the performance of your competitors and other organizations with similar offerings?
<--- Score

12. What needs improvement? Why?
<--- Score

13. What is telecom providers risk?
<--- Score

14. Is there a cost/benefit analysis of optimal solution(s)?
<--- Score

15. What resources are required for the improvement efforts?
<--- Score

16. Is the optimal solution selected based on testing and analysis?
<--- Score

17. Who are the people involved in developing and implementing telecom providers?
<--- Score

18. Who controls the risk?
<--- Score

19. What does the 'should be' process map/design look like?
<--- Score

20. Are events managed to resolution?
<--- Score

21. What were the criteria for evaluating a telecom providers pilot?
<--- Score

22. What is the team's contingency plan for potential problems occurring in implementation?
<--- Score

23. How is knowledge sharing about risk management improved?

<--- Score

24. What telecom providers improvements can be made?
<--- Score

25. What can you do to improve?
<--- Score

26. Who will be responsible for making the decisions to include or exclude requested changes once telecom providers is underway?
<--- Score

27. Would you develop a telecom providers Communication Strategy?
<--- Score

28. Risk factors: what are the characteristics of telecom providers that make it risky?
<--- Score

29. Why improve in the first place?
<--- Score

30. What are the expected telecom providers results?
<--- Score

31. Was a telecom providers charter developed?
<--- Score

32. How do you manage and improve your telecom providers work systems to deliver customer value and achieve organizational success and sustainability?
<--- Score

33. Is the telecom providers documentation thorough?

<--- Score

34. Are decisions made in a timely manner?

<--- Score

35. For estimation problems, how do you develop an estimation statement?

<--- Score

36. How do you improve productivity?

<--- Score

37. What are the telecom providers security risks?

<--- Score

38. What improvements have been achieved?

<--- Score

39. Can the solution be designed and implemented within an acceptable time period?

<--- Score

40. What alternative responses are available to manage risk?

<--- Score

41. What tools were used to tap into the creativity and encourage 'outside the box' thinking?

<--- Score

42. Who will be using the results of the measurement activities?

<--- Score

43. For decision problems, how do you develop a decision statement?

<--- Score

44. How does your organization evaluate strategic telecom providers success?

<--- Score

45. If you could go back in time five years, what decision would you make differently? What is your best guess as to what decision you're making today you might regret five years from now?

<--- Score

46. Where do the telecom providers decisions reside?

<--- Score

47. Who manages supplier risk management in your organization?

<--- Score

48. Have you identified breakpoints and/or risk tolerances that will trigger broad consideration of a potential need for intervention or modification of strategy?

<--- Score

49. Who makes the telecom providers decisions in your organization?

<--- Score

50. How significant is the improvement in the eyes of the end user?

<--- Score

51. How do you measure risk?
<--- Score

52. When you map the key players in your own work and the types/domains of relationships with them, which relationships do you find easy and which challenging, and why?
<--- Score

53. What is the implementation plan?
<--- Score

54. How do you improve telecom providers service perception, and satisfaction?
<--- Score

55. In the past few months, what is the smallest change you have made that has had the biggest positive result? What was it about that small change that produced the large return?
<--- Score

56. What is the telecom providers's sustainability risk?
<--- Score

57. Is the measure of success for telecom providers understandable to a variety of people?
<--- Score

58. What do you want to improve?
<--- Score

59. Do you combine technical expertise with business knowledge and telecom providers Key topics include lifecycles, development approaches, requirements and how to make a business case?

<--- Score

60. How will you recognize and celebrate results?
<--- Score

61. Can you identify any significant risks or exposures to telecom providers third- parties (vendors, service providers, alliance partners etc) that concern you?
<--- Score

62. Risk events: what are the things that could go wrong?
<--- Score

63. Which of the recognised risks out of all risks can be most likely transferred?
<--- Score

64. Risk Identification: What are the possible risk events your organization faces in relation to telecom providers?
<--- Score

65. Is there a small-scale pilot for proposed improvement(s)? What conclusions were drawn from the outcomes of a pilot?
<--- Score

66. How will you know that you have improved?
<--- Score

67. What went well, what should change, what can improve?
<--- Score

68. Is the telecom providers solution sustainable?

<--- Score

69. How do you measure improved telecom providers service perception, and satisfaction?
<--- Score

70. Is there a high likelihood that any recommendations will achieve their intended results?
<--- Score

71. Is there any other telecom providers solution?
<--- Score

72. What attendant changes will need to be made to ensure that the solution is successful?
<--- Score

73. How will you know when its improved?
<--- Score

74. How do you go about comparing telecom providers approaches/solutions?
<--- Score

75. What area needs the greatest improvement?
<--- Score

76. What are the concrete telecom providers results?
<--- Score

77. Is risk periodically assessed?
<--- Score

78. What is the magnitude of the improvements?
<--- Score

79. Do you need to do a usability evaluation?
<--- Score

80. What assumptions are made about the solution and approach?
<--- Score

81. Is supporting telecom providers documentation required?
<--- Score

82. What were the underlying assumptions on the cost-benefit analysis?
<--- Score

83. Who are the key stakeholders for the telecom providers evaluation?
<--- Score

84. Will the controls trigger any other risks?
<--- Score

85. Do you cover the five essential competencies: Communication, Collaboration,Innovation, Adaptability, and Leadership that improve an organizations ability to leverage the new telecom providers in a volatile global economy?
<--- Score

86. How risky is your organization?
<--- Score

87. What are the implications of the one critical telecom providers decision 10 minutes, 10 months, and 10 years from now?

<--- Score

88. Are procedures documented for managing telecom providers risks?
<--- Score

89. What lessons, if any, from a pilot were incorporated into the design of the full-scale solution?
<--- Score

90. What risks do you need to manage?
<--- Score

91. How do you improve your likelihood of success ?
<--- Score

92. How do you manage telecom providers risk?
<--- Score

93. Is the implementation plan designed?
<--- Score

94. What communications are necessary to support the implementation of the solution?
<--- Score

95. How will you know that a change is an improvement?
<--- Score

96. How do you link measurement and risk?
<--- Score

97. Who controls key decisions that will be made?
<--- Score

98. How do you define the solutions' scope?
<--- Score

99. Who are the telecom providers decision-makers?
<--- Score

100. What tools were most useful during the improve phase?
<--- Score

101. What tools were used to evaluate the potential solutions?
<--- Score

102. To what extent does management recognize telecom providers as a tool to increase the results?
<--- Score

103. What actually has to improve and by how much?
<--- Score

104. How can you improve performance?
<--- Score

105. How are telecom providers risks managed?
<--- Score

106. Is any telecom providers documentation required?
<--- Score

107. What should a proof of concept or pilot accomplish?
<--- Score

108. How scalable is your telecom providers solution?

<--- Score

109. What criteria will you use to assess your telecom providers risks?
<--- Score

110. Who manages telecom providers risk?
<--- Score

111. What strategies for telecom providers improvement are successful?
<--- Score

112. Was a pilot designed for the proposed solution(s)?
<--- Score

113. What is telecom providers's impact on utilizing the best solution(s)?
<--- Score

114. telecom providers risk decisions: whose call Is It?
<--- Score

115. How do you decide how much to remunerate an employee?
<--- Score

116. Do you have the optimal project management team structure?
<--- Score

117. How do you deal with telecom providers risk?
<--- Score

118. How do you keep improving telecom providers?

<--- Score

119. Who should make the telecom providers decisions?
<--- Score

120. Does a good decision guarantee a good outcome?
<--- Score

121. Where do you need telecom providers improvement?
<--- Score

122. How do you mitigate telecom providers risk?
<--- Score

123. Do those selected for the telecom providers team have a good general understanding of what telecom providers is all about?
<--- Score

124. Do vendor agreements bring new compliance risk ?
<--- Score

125. What error proofing will be done to address some of the discrepancies observed in the 'as is' process?
<--- Score

126. Is the solution technically practical?
<--- Score

127. At what point will vulnerability assessments be performed once telecom providers is put into production (e.g., ongoing Risk Management after

implementation)?
<--- Score

128. How can the phases of telecom providers development be identified?
<--- Score

129. What to do with the results or outcomes of measurements?
<--- Score

130. Were any criteria developed to assist the team in testing and evaluating potential solutions?
<--- Score

131. How can skill-level changes improve telecom providers?
<--- Score

Add up total points for this section:
_____ = Total points for this section

Divided by: _____ (number of statements answered) = _____
Average score for this section

Transfer your score to the telecom providers Index at the beginning of the Self-Assessment.

CRITERION #6: CONTROL:

INTENT: Implement the practical solution. Maintain the performance and correct possible complications.

In my belief, the answer to this question is clearly defined:

5 Strongly Agree

4 Agree

3 Neutral

2 Disagree

1 Strongly Disagree

1. Can you adapt and adjust to changing telecom providers situations?
<--- Score

2. Is new knowledge gained imbedded in the response plan?
<--- Score

3. Has the telecom providers value of standards been

quantified?
<--- Score

4. How will the day-to-day responsibilities for monitoring and continual improvement be transferred from the improvement team to the process owner?
<--- Score

5. How do you plan for the cost of succession?
<--- Score

6. What other systems, operations, processes, and infrastructures (hiring practices, staffing, training, incentives/rewards, metrics/dashboards/scorecards, etc.) need updates, additions, changes, or deletions in order to facilitate knowledge transfer and improvements?
<--- Score

7. Do you monitor the effectiveness of your telecom providers activities?
<--- Score

8. Where do ideas that reach policy makers and planners as proposals for telecom providers strengthening and reform actually originate?
<--- Score

9. Does the response plan contain a definite closed loop continual improvement scheme (e.g., plan-do-check-act)?
<--- Score

10. Are the planned controls in place?
<--- Score

11. Does the telecom providers performance meet the customer's requirements?
<--- Score

12. Is a response plan in place for when the input, process, or output measures indicate an 'out-of-control' condition?
<--- Score

13. How do your controls stack up?
<--- Score

14. Is reporting being used or needed?
<--- Score

15. How will the process owner and team be able to hold the gains?
<--- Score

16. Do you monitor the telecom providers decisions made and fine tune them as they evolve?
<--- Score

17. How will input, process, and output variables be checked to detect for sub-optimal conditions?
<--- Score

18. Who will be in control?
<--- Score

19. How do you encourage people to take control and responsibility?
<--- Score

20. Is knowledge gained on process shared and

institutionalized?
<--- Score

21. Are the telecom providers standards challenging?
<--- Score

22. Is a response plan established and deployed?
<--- Score

23. Is there an action plan in case of emergencies?
<--- Score

24. Is there a standardized process?
<--- Score

25. What should the next improvement project be that is related to telecom providers?
<--- Score

26. In the case of a telecom providers project, the criteria for the audit derive from implementation objectives, an audit of a telecom providers project involves assessing whether the recommendations outlined for implementation have been met, can you track that any telecom providers project is implemented as planned, and is it working?
<--- Score

27. Has the improved process and its steps been standardized?
<--- Score

28. How will telecom providers decisions be made and monitored?
<--- Score

29. Is there a documented and implemented monitoring plan?
<--- Score

30. Is there a recommended audit plan for routine surveillance inspections of telecom providers's gains?
<--- Score

31. How do you plan on providing proper recognition and disclosure of supporting companies?
<--- Score

32. How might the group capture best practices and lessons learned so as to leverage improvements?
<--- Score

33. How widespread is its use?
<--- Score

34. Are new process steps, standards, and documentation ingrained into normal operations?
<--- Score

35. Will existing staff require re-training, for example, to learn new business processes?
<--- Score

36. What other areas of the group might benefit from the telecom providers team's improvements, knowledge, and learning?
<--- Score

37. Who controls critical resources?
<--- Score

38. How can you best use all of your knowledge

repositories to enhance learning and sharing?
<--- Score

39. What is the control/monitoring plan?
<--- Score

40. How is telecom providers project cost planned, managed, monitored?
<--- Score

41. What is the best design framework for telecom providers organization now that, in a post industrial-age if the top-down, command and control model is no longer relevant?
<--- Score

42. What are the known security controls?
<--- Score

43. Are controls in place and consistently applied?
<--- Score

44. What do you measure to verify effectiveness gains?
<--- Score

45. Have new or revised work instructions resulted?
<--- Score

46. Is the telecom providers test/monitoring cost justified?
<--- Score

47. Who is going to spread your message?
<--- Score

48. How is change control managed?
<--- Score

49. Are the planned controls working?
<--- Score

50. Is there documentation that will support the successful operation of the improvement?
<--- Score

51. What is your theory of human motivation, and how does your compensation plan fit with that view?
<--- Score

52. Does telecom providers appropriately measure and monitor risk?
<--- Score

53. Implementation Planning: is a pilot needed to test the changes before a full roll out occurs?
<--- Score

54. How will the process owner verify improvement in present and future sigma levels, process capabilities?
<--- Score

55. How do you spread information?
<--- Score

56. Are suggested corrective/restorative actions indicated on the response plan for known causes to problems that might surface?
<--- Score

57. Does a troubleshooting guide exist or is it needed?
<--- Score

58. What is the standard for acceptable telecom providers performance?

<--- Score

59. What are the key elements of your telecom providers performance improvement system, including your evaluation, organizational learning, and innovation processes?

<--- Score

60. Who is the telecom providers process owner?

<--- Score

61. How do you establish and deploy modified action plans if circumstances require a shift in plans and rapid execution of new plans?

<--- Score

62. Is there a telecom providers Communication plan covering who needs to get what information when?

<--- Score

63. Do the telecom providers decisions you make today help people and the planet tomorrow?

<--- Score

64. Is there a control plan in place for sustaining improvements (short and long-term)?

<--- Score

65. How will report readings be checked to effectively monitor performance?

<--- Score

66. Will the team be available to assist members in planning investigations?
<--- Score

67. Is there a transfer of ownership and knowledge to process owner and process team tasked with the responsibilities.
<--- Score

68. Can support from partners be adjusted?
<--- Score

69. What are the critical parameters to watch?
<--- Score

70. Are you measuring, monitoring and predicting telecom providers activities to optimize operations and profitability, and enhancing outcomes?
<--- Score

71. Does job training on the documented procedures need to be part of the process team's education and training?
<--- Score

72. How do controls support value?
<--- Score

73. What adjustments to the strategies are needed?
<--- Score

74. What quality tools were useful in the control phase?
<--- Score

75. What telecom providers standards are applicable?

<--- Score

76. What key inputs and outputs are being measured on an ongoing basis?
<--- Score

77. Will any special training be provided for results interpretation?
<--- Score

78. Are operating procedures consistent?
<--- Score

79. How do senior leaders actions reflect a commitment to the organizations telecom providers values?
<--- Score

80. What do your reports reflect?
<--- Score

81. How do you select, collect, align, and integrate telecom providers data and information for tracking daily operations and overall organizational performance, including progress relative to strategic objectives and action plans?
<--- Score

82. How will you measure your QA plan's effectiveness?
<--- Score

83. What can you control?
<--- Score

84. What are you attempting to measure/monitor?

<--- Score

85. Who has control over resources?
<--- Score

86. Against what alternative is success being measured?
<--- Score

87. Are documented procedures clear and easy to follow for the operators?
<--- Score

88. You may have created your quality measures at a time when you lacked resources, technology wasn't up to the required standard, or low service levels were the industry norm. Have those circumstances changed?
<--- Score

89. What are your results for key measures or indicators of the accomplishment of your telecom providers strategy and action plans, including building and strengthening core competencies?
<--- Score

90. Act/Adjust: What Do you Need to Do Differently?
<--- Score

91. How likely is the current telecom providers plan to come in on schedule or on budget?
<--- Score

92. Will your goals reflect your program budget?
<--- Score

93. How will new or emerging customer needs/ requirements be checked/communicated to orient the process toward meeting the new specifications and continually reducing variation?
<--- Score

94. What is the recommended frequency of auditing?
<--- Score

95. What are customers monitoring?
<--- Score

96. Are there documented procedures?
<--- Score

97. Who sets the telecom providers standards?
<--- Score

Add up total points for this section:
_ _ _ _ _ = Total points for this section

Divided by: _ _ _ _ _ _ (number of statements answered) = _ _ _ _ _ _
Average score for this section

Transfer your score to the telecom providers Index at the beginning of the Self-Assessment.

CRITERION #7: SUSTAIN:

INTENT: Retain the benefits.

In my belief, the answer to this question is clearly defined:

5 Strongly Agree

4 Agree

3 Neutral

2 Disagree

1 Strongly Disagree

1. What are the usability implications of telecom providers actions?
<--- Score

2. What would you recommend your friend do if he/she were facing this dilemma?
<--- Score

3. Are the assumptions believable and achievable?
<--- Score

4. What is your BATNA (best alternative to a negotiated agreement)?

<--- Score

5. When information truly is ubiquitous, when reach and connectivity are completely global, when computing resources are infinite, and when a whole new set of impossibilities are not only possible, but happening, what will that do to your business?

<--- Score

6. How can you become more high-tech but still be high touch?

<--- Score

7. Has implementation been effective in reaching specified objectives so far?

<--- Score

8. To whom do you add value?

<--- Score

9. How do you engage the workforce, in addition to satisfying them?

<--- Score

10. Who uses your product in ways you never expected?

<--- Score

11. Who is responsible for ensuring appropriate resources (time, people and money) are allocated to telecom providers?

<--- Score

12. Where can you break convention?
<--- Score

13. Is it economical; do you have the time and money?
<--- Score

14. Why should people listen to you?
<--- Score

15. What new services of functionality will be implemented next with telecom providers ?
<--- Score

16. Instead of going to current contacts for new ideas, what if you reconnected with dormant contacts-- the people you used to know? If you were going reactivate a dormant tie, who would it be?
<--- Score

17. What do we do when new problems arise?
<--- Score

18. What are the barriers to increased telecom providers production?
<--- Score

19. Why is telecom providers important for you now?
<--- Score

20. How do you keep the momentum going?
<--- Score

21. What have been your experiences in defining long range telecom providers goals?

<--- Score

22. Can you break it down?
<--- Score

23. Are you maintaining a past–present–future perspective throughout the telecom providers discussion?
<--- Score

24. What telecom providers skills are most important?
<--- Score

25. What could happen if you do not do it?
<--- Score

26. Who are four people whose careers you have enhanced?
<--- Score

27. Why do and why don't your customers like your organization?
<--- Score

28. What is the purpose of telecom providers in relation to the mission?
<--- Score

29. If your company went out of business tomorrow, would anyone who doesn't get a paycheck here care?
<--- Score

30. What is it like to work for you?
<--- Score

31. What telecom providers modifications can you

make work for you?
<--- Score

32. What role does communication play in the success or failure of a telecom providers project?
<--- Score

33. How do you assess the telecom providers pitfalls that are inherent in implementing it?
<--- Score

34. How do you govern and fulfill your societal responsibilities?
<--- Score

35. What are the short and long-term telecom providers goals?
<--- Score

36. What does your signature ensure?
<--- Score

37. How do you set telecom providers stretch targets and how do you get people to not only participate in setting these stretch targets but also that they strive to achieve these?
<--- Score

38. Do you know who is a friend or a foe?
<--- Score

39. How do you keep records, of what?
<--- Score

40. What are the essentials of internal telecom providers management?

<--- Score

41. Is there any reason to believe the opposite of my current belief?
<--- Score

42. What is the recommended frequency of auditing?
<--- Score

43. How do you maintain telecom providers's Integrity?
<--- Score

44. How will you know that the telecom providers project has been successful?
<--- Score

45. If there were zero limitations, what would you do differently?
<--- Score

46. How do you transition from the baseline to the target?
<--- Score

47. Do you think telecom providers accomplishes the goals you expect it to accomplish?
<--- Score

48. What are the rules and assumptions your industry operates under? What if the opposite were true?
<--- Score

49. How is implementation research currently incorporated into each of your goals?

<--- Score

50. Which functions and people interact with the supplier and or customer?
<--- Score

51. Are the criteria for selecting recommendations stated?
<--- Score

52. How much contingency will be available in the budget?
<--- Score

53. How do you foster the skills, knowledge, talents, attributes, and characteristics you want to have?
<--- Score

54. What is the kind of project structure that would be appropriate for your telecom providers project, should it be formal and complex, or can it be less formal and relatively simple?
<--- Score

55. Who are your customers?
<--- Score

56. How are you doing compared to your industry?
<--- Score

57. Are assumptions made in telecom providers stated explicitly?
<--- Score

58. If you do not follow, then how to lead?
<--- Score

59. If you had to leave your organization for a year and the only communication you could have with employees/colleagues was a single paragraph, what would you write?
<--- Score

60. Are you satisfied with your current role? If not, what is missing from it?
<--- Score

61. What are specific telecom providers rules to follow?
<--- Score

62. Who will manage the integration of tools?
<--- Score

63. Who have you, as a company, historically been when you've been at your best?
<--- Score

64. Who do you think the world wants your organization to be?
<--- Score

65. What counts that you are not counting?
<--- Score

66. What is the estimated value of the project?
<--- Score

67. Is there any existing telecom providers governance structure?
<--- Score

68. Whose voice (department, ethnic group, women, older workers, etc) might you have missed hearing from in your company, and how might you amplify this voice to create positive momentum for your business?
<--- Score

69. Are you paying enough attention to the partners your company depends on to succeed?
<--- Score

70. How do you make it meaningful in connecting telecom providers with what users do day-to-day?
<--- Score

71. Would you rather sell to knowledgeable and informed customers or to uninformed customers?
<--- Score

72. What should you stop doing?
<--- Score

73. How do you go about securing telecom providers?
<--- Score

74. Who is the main stakeholder, with ultimate responsibility for driving telecom providers forward?
<--- Score

75. What one word do you want to own in the minds of your customers, employees, and partners?
<--- Score

76. What are the top 3 things at the forefront of your telecom providers agendas for the next 3 years?

<--- Score

77. What is your competitive advantage?
<--- Score

78. What is something you believe that nearly no one agrees with you on?
<--- Score

79. Who is responsible for errors?
<--- Score

80. Ask yourself: how would you do this work if you only had one staff member to do it?
<--- Score

81. How will you ensure you get what you expected?
<--- Score

82. How do you cross-sell and up-sell your telecom providers success?
<--- Score

83. What are the business goals telecom providers is aiming to achieve?
<--- Score

84. Is your basic point _____ or _____?
<--- Score

85. In a project to restructure telecom providers outcomes, which stakeholders would you involve?
<--- Score

86. What would have to be true for the option on the table to be the best possible choice?

<--- Score

87. Can you maintain your growth without detracting from the factors that have contributed to your success?
<--- Score

88. What will be the consequences to the stakeholder (financial, reputation etc) if telecom providers does not go ahead or fails to deliver the objectives?
<--- Score

89. What projects are going on in the organization today, and what resources are those projects using from the resource pools?
<--- Score

90. Do you have enough freaky customers in your portfolio pushing you to the limit day in and day out?
<--- Score

91. What are you trying to prove to yourself, and how might it be hijacking your life and business success?
<--- Score

92. What are your most important goals for the strategic telecom providers objectives?
<--- Score

93. What is your telecom providers strategy?
<--- Score

94. How do you accomplish your long range telecom providers goals?

<--- Score

95. What are your personal philosophies regarding telecom providers and how do they influence your work?
<--- Score

96. Who will provide the final approval of telecom providers deliverables?
<--- Score

97. How do you provide a safe environment -physically and emotionally?
<--- Score

98. How can you incorporate support to ensure safe and effective use of telecom providers into the services that you provide?
<--- Score

99. If your customer were your grandmother, would you tell her to buy what you're selling?
<--- Score

100. What are internal and external telecom providers relations?
<--- Score

101. What management system can you use to leverage the telecom providers experience, ideas, and concerns of the people closest to the work to be done?
<--- Score

102. Are you / should you be revolutionary or evolutionary?

<--- Score

103. Is maximizing telecom providers protection the same as minimizing telecom providers loss?
<--- Score

104. How do you deal with telecom providers changes?
<--- Score

105. How do senior leaders deploy your organizations vision and values through your leadership system, to the workforce, to key suppliers and partners, and to customers and other stakeholders, as appropriate?
<--- Score

106. Is a telecom providers team work effort in place?
<--- Score

107. What may be the consequences for the performance of an organization if all stakeholders are not consulted regarding telecom providers?
<--- Score

108. Have new benefits been realized?
<--- Score

109. How do you listen to customers to obtain actionable information?
<--- Score

110. What are the gaps in your knowledge and experience?
<--- Score

111. How can you negotiate telecom providers successfully with a stubborn boss, an irate client, or a deceitful coworker?

<--- Score

112. Do you have the right people on the bus?

<--- Score

113. What potential megatrends could make your business model obsolete?

<--- Score

114. What must you excel at?

<--- Score

115. How do you determine the key elements that affect telecom providers workforce satisfaction, how are these elements determined for different workforce groups and segments?

<--- Score

116. If no one would ever find out about your accomplishments, how would you lead differently?

<--- Score

117. How will you insure seamless interoperability of telecom providers moving forward?

<--- Score

118. Why not do telecom providers?

<--- Score

119. What are the challenges?

<--- Score

120. What knowledge, skills and characteristics mark a good telecom providers project manager?
<--- Score

121. What relationships among telecom providers trends do you perceive?
<--- Score

122. How do you track customer value, profitability or financial return, organizational success, and sustainability?
<--- Score

123. Why will customers want to buy your organizations products/services?
<--- Score

124. How does telecom providers integrate with other stakeholder initiatives?
<--- Score

125. Think of your telecom providers project, what are the main functions?
<--- Score

126. Who, on the executive team or the board, has spoken to a customer recently?
<--- Score

127. How do you create buy-in?
<--- Score

128. What is the overall business strategy?
<--- Score

129. Who do we want your customers to become?

<--- Score

130. Who is responsible for telecom providers?
<--- Score

131. What are the performance and scale of the telecom providers tools?
<--- Score

132. What are you challenging?
<--- Score

133. Are your responses positive or negative?
<--- Score

134. Which telecom providers goals are the most important?
<--- Score

135. What is your question? Why?
<--- Score

136. What you are going to do to affect the numbers?
<--- Score

137. What are strategies for increasing support and reducing opposition?
<--- Score

138. What trouble can you get into?
<--- Score

139. Can you do all this work?
<--- Score

140. If you weren't already in this business, would

you enter it today? And if not, what are you going to do about it?
<--- Score

141. How likely is it that a customer would recommend your company to a friend or colleague?
<--- Score

142. What business benefits will telecom providers goals deliver if achieved?
<--- Score

143. Do you have past telecom providers successes?
<--- Score

144. Are you relevant? Will you be relevant five years from now? Ten?
<--- Score

145. Whom among your colleagues do you trust, and for what?
<--- Score

146. If you had to rebuild your organization without any traditional competitive advantages (i.e., no killer technology, promising research, innovative product/service delivery model, etcetera), how would your people have to approach their work and collaborate together in order to create the necessary conditions for success?
<--- Score

147. Which models, tools and techniques are necessary?
<--- Score

148. Is a telecom providers breakthrough on the horizon?
<--- Score

149. Do you have an implicit bias for capital investments over people investments?
<--- Score

150. What was the last experiment you ran?
<--- Score

151. What is your formula for success in telecom providers ?
<--- Score

152. Is telecom providers dependent on the successful delivery of a current project?
<--- Score

153. What is the big telecom providers idea?
<--- Score

154. How important is telecom providers to the user organizations mission?
<--- Score

155. Marketing budgets are tighter, consumers are more skeptical, and social media has changed forever the way we talk about telecom providers, how do you gain traction?
<--- Score

156. How do you stay inspired?
<--- Score

157. Will it be accepted by users?
<--- Score

158. What current systems have to be understood and/or changed?
<--- Score

159. How much does telecom providers help?
<--- Score

160. In retrospect, of the projects that you pulled the plug on, what percent do you wish had been allowed to keep going, and what percent do you wish had ended earlier?
<--- Score

161. How can you become the company that would put you out of business?
<--- Score

162. What have you done to protect your business from competitive encroachment?
<--- Score

163. In the past year, what have you done (or could you have done) to increase the accurate perception of your company/brand as ethical and honest?
<--- Score

164. What is the overall talent health of your organization as a whole at senior levels, and for each organization reporting to a member of the Senior Leadership Team?
<--- Score

165. Are there any activities that you can take off your

to do list?
<--- Score

166. What information is critical to your organization that your executives are ignoring?
<--- Score

167. Is telecom providers realistic, or are you setting yourself up for failure?
<--- Score

168. What are the long-term telecom providers goals?
<--- Score

169. Who will be responsible for deciding whether telecom providers goes ahead or not after the initial investigations?
<--- Score

170. Do telecom providers rules make a reasonable demand on a users capabilities?
<--- Score

171. How do customers see your organization?
<--- Score

172. Do you think you know, or do you know you know ?
<--- Score

173. How do you manage telecom providers Knowledge Management (KM)?
<--- Score

174. What is a feasible sequencing of reform initiatives over time?

<--- Score

175. At what moment would you think; Will I get fired?
<--- Score

176. How do you foster innovation?
<--- Score

177. Who are the key stakeholders?
<--- Score

178. How will you motivate the stakeholders with the least vested interest?
<--- Score

179. How do you lead with telecom providers in mind?
<--- Score

180. What trophy do you want on your mantle?
<--- Score

181. Why should you adopt a telecom providers framework?
<--- Score

182. Are new benefits received and understood?
<--- Score

183. Political -is anyone trying to undermine this project?
<--- Score

184. Can the schedule be done in the given time?
<--- Score

185. What are the key enablers to make this telecom providers move?
<--- Score

186. What stupid rule would you most like to kill?
<--- Score

187. What goals did you miss?
<--- Score

188. If you got fired and a new hire took your place, what would she do different?
<--- Score

189. What is the funding source for this project?
<--- Score

190. If you were responsible for initiating and implementing major changes in your organization, what steps might you take to ensure acceptance of those changes?
<--- Score

191. Is your strategy driving your strategy? Or is the way in which you allocate resources driving your strategy?
<--- Score

192. Operational - will it work?
<--- Score

193. What is the craziest thing you can do?
<--- Score

194. Do you feel that more should be done in the telecom providers area?

<--- Score

195. What is an unauthorized commitment?
<--- Score

196. Will there be any necessary staff changes
(redundancies or new hires)?
<--- Score

197. Who else should you help?
<--- Score

198. Are you making progress, and are you making
progress as telecom providers leaders?
<--- Score

199. Why is it important to have senior management
support for a telecom providers project?
<--- Score

200. Is the telecom providers organization completing
tasks effectively and efficiently?
<--- Score

201. What is effective telecom providers?
<--- Score

202. Who will determine interim and final deadlines?
<--- Score

**203. If you find that you havent accomplished one
of the goals for one of the steps of the telecom
providers strategy, what will you do to fix it?**
<--- Score

204. Is the impact that telecom providers has shown?

<--- Score

205. Were lessons learned captured and communicated?
<--- Score

206. What unique value proposition (UVP) do you offer?
<--- Score

207. Which individuals, teams or departments will be involved in telecom providers?
<--- Score

208. Are you changing as fast as the world around you?
<--- Score

209. What are current telecom providers paradigms?
<--- Score

210. What did you miss in the interview for the worst hire you ever made?
<--- Score

211. Are you using a design thinking approach and integrating Innovation, telecom providers Experience, and Brand Value?
<--- Score

212. What happens when a new employee joins the organization?
<--- Score

213. What is the source of the strategies for telecom providers strengthening and reform?

<--- Score

214. What is the range of capabilities?
<--- Score

215. Are all key stakeholders present at all Structured Walkthroughs?
<--- Score

216. Have benefits been optimized with all key stakeholders?
<--- Score

Add up total points for this section:
_____ = Total points for this section

Divided by: _____ (number of statements answered) = _____
Average score for this section

Transfer your score to the telecom providers Index at the beginning of the Self-Assessment.

Telecom Providers and Managing Projects, Criteria for Project Managers:

1.0 Initiating Process Group: Telecom Providers

1. How well did the chosen processes fit the needs of the Telecom Providers project?

2. Who is performing the work of the Telecom Providers project?

3. What do you need to do?

4. Professionals want to know what is expected from them what are the deliverables?

5. Who is involved in each phase?

6. Do you know the Telecom Providers projects goal, purpose and objectives?

7. Which six sigma dmaic phase focuses on why and how defects and errors occur?

8. When are the deliverables to be generated in each phase?

9. Just how important is your work to the overall success of the Telecom Providers project?

10. What input will you be required to provide the Telecom Providers project team?

11. Who are the Telecom Providers project stakeholders?

12. Who supports, improves, and oversees

standardized processes related to the Telecom Providers projects program?

13. What will you do to minimize the impact should a risk event occur?

14. Are identified risks being monitored properly, are new risks arising during the Telecom Providers project or are foreseen risks occurring?

15. What are the short and long term implications?

16. If the risk event occurs, what will you do?

17. Contingency planning. if a risk event occurs, what will you do?

18. What technical work to do in each phase?

19. If action is called for, what form should it take?

20. Realistic - are the desired results expressed in a way that the team will be motivated and believe that the required level of involvement will be obtained?

1.1 Project Charter: Telecom Providers

21. Name and describe the elements that deal with providing the detail?

22. If finished, on what date did it finish?

23. What is the business need?

24. Who is the Telecom Providers project Manager?

25. How much?

26. Environmental stewardship and sustainability considerations: what is the process that will be used to ensure compliance with the environmental stewardship policy?

27. Telecom Providers project objective statement: what must the Telecom Providers project do?

28. Telecom Providers project background: what is the primary motivation for this Telecom Providers project?

29. What outcome, in measureable terms, are you hoping to accomplish?

30. Why Outsource?

31. Who is the sponsor?

32. Major high-level milestone targets: what events measure progress?

33. Market – identify products market, including whether it is outside of the objective: what is the purpose of the program or Telecom Providers project?

34. Why executive support?

35. Why is a Telecom Providers project Charter used?

36. Why have you chosen the aim you have set forth?

37. Are you building in-house ?

38. How will you learn more about the process or system you are trying to improve?

39. Review the general mission What system will be affected by the improvement efforts?

40. Will this replace an existing product?

1.2 Stakeholder Register: Telecom Providers

41. What & Why?

42. How big is the gap?

43. How will reports be created?

44. What opportunities exist to provide communications?

45. Is your organization ready for change?

46. Who wants to talk about Security?

47. How much influence do they have on the Telecom Providers project?

48. Who is managing stakeholder engagement?

49. What are the major Telecom Providers project milestones requiring communications or providing communications opportunities?

50. How should employers make voices heard?

51. Who are the stakeholders?

52. What is the power of the stakeholder?

1.3 Stakeholder Analysis Matrix: Telecom Providers

53. What do people from other organizations see as your organizations weaknesses?

54. If the baseline is now, and if its improved it will be better than now?

55. Tactics: eg, surprise, major contracts?

56. Technology development and innovation?

57. What is the issue at stake?

58. How will the Telecom Providers project benefit them?

59. How to involve media?

60. Which conditions out of the control of the management are crucial to contribute for the achievement of the development objective?

61. What is the relationship among stakeholders?

62. Competitors vulnerabilities?

63. What advantages do your organizations stakeholders have?

64. How to measure the achievement of the Immediate Objective?

65. Are there different rules or organizational models for men and women?

66. Who will be affected by the Telecom Providers project?

67. Arena: in what fields are the actors active, where are they present?

68. Are you working on the right risks?

69. Who will be affected by the Telecom Providers project?

70. Who has been involved in the area (thematic or geographic) in the past?

71. Does your organization have bad debt or cash-flow problems?

72. Management cover, succession?

2.0 Planning Process Group: Telecom Providers

73. To what extent has the intervention strategy been adapted to the areas of intervention in which it is being implemented?

74. What input will you be required to provide the Telecom Providers project team?

75. On which process should team members spend the most time?

76. What should you do next?

77. Have more efficient (sensitive) and appropriate measures been adopted to respond to the political and socio-cultural problems identified?

78. Is the Telecom Providers project supported by national and/or local organizations?

79. How can you make your needs known?

80. How well will the chosen processes produce the expected results?

81. How are the principles of aid effectiveness (ownership, alignment, management for development results and mutual responsibility) being applied in the Telecom Providers project?

82. In what way has the Telecom Providers project

come up with innovative measures for problem-solving?

83. When will the Telecom Providers project be done?

84. You are creating your WBS and find that you keep decomposing tasks into smaller and smaller units. How can you tell when you are done?

85. If task x starts two days late, what is the effect on the Telecom Providers project end date?

86. The Telecom Providers project charter is created in which Telecom Providers project management process group?

87. How will you know you did it?

88. If you are late, will anybody notice?

89. What is a Software Development Life Cycle (SDLC)?

90. What business situation is being addressed?

91. Is the duration of the program sufficient to ensure a cycle that will Telecom Providers project the sustainability of the interventions?

92. Is the pace of implementing the products of the program ensuring the completeness of the results of the Telecom Providers project?

2.1 Project Management Plan: Telecom Providers

93. Are the proposed Telecom Providers project purposes different than a previously authorized Telecom Providers project?

94. What is risk management?

95. What are the assumptions?

96. If the Telecom Providers project is complex or scope is specialized, do you have appropriate and/or qualified staff available to perform the tasks?

97. What would you do differently?

98. Is the appropriate plan selected based on your organizations objectives and evaluation criteria expressed in Principles and Guidelines policies?

99. What if, for example, the positive direction and vision of your organization causes expected trends to change resulting in greater need than expected?

100. Are calculations and results of analyzes essentially correct?

101. When is a Telecom Providers project management plan created?

102. What is the justification?

103. What are the known stakeholder requirements?

104. What data/reports/tools/etc. do your PMs need?

105. Will you add a schedule and diagram?

106. What are the training needs?

107. What goes into your Telecom Providers project Charter?

108. What should you drop in order to add something new?

109. How do you manage time?

110. Is mitigation authorized or recommended?

111. When is the Telecom Providers project management plan created?

2.2 Scope Management Plan: Telecom Providers

112. Are the Telecom Providers project team members located locally to the users/stakeholders?

113. Is there a Telecom Providers project organization chart showing the reporting relationships and responsibilities for each position?

114. Describe the process for accepting the Telecom Providers project deliverables. Will the Telecom Providers project deliverables become accepted in writing?

115. Have the personnel with the necessary skills and competence been identified and has agreement for participation in the Telecom Providers project been reached with the appropriate management?

116. What are the acceptance criteria (process and criteria to be met for key stakeholder acceptance) and who is authorized to sign off?

117. What went wrong?

118. Is the quality assurance team identified?

119. Has the business need been clearly defined?

120. Has allowance been made for vacations, holidays, training (learning time for each team member), staff promotions & staff turnovers?

121. Are you meeting with stake holders and team members?

122. Sensitivity analysis?

123. Has a sponsor been identified?

124. Is there general agreement & acceptance of the current status and progress of the Telecom Providers project?

125. Have reserves been created to address risks?

126. How much money have you spent?

127. Are you spending the right amount of money for specific tasks?

128. What is the relative power of the Telecom Providers project manager?

129. Has a resource management plan been created?

130. Are corrective actions taken when actual results are substantially different from detailed Telecom Providers project plan (variances)?

131. Have Telecom Providers project success criteria been defined?

2.3 Requirements Management Plan: Telecom Providers

132. Who will do the reporting and to whom will reports be delivered?

133. Will you document changes to requirements?

134. Do you have price sheets and a methodology for determining the total proposal cost?

135. Who will finally present the work or product(s) for acceptance?

136. How will the information be distributed?

137. Will you have access to stakeholders when you need them?

138. Should you include sub-activities?

139. Is the change control process documented?

140. After the requirements are gathered and set forth on the requirements register, theyre little more than a laundry list of items. Some may be duplicates, some might conflict with others and some will be too broad or too vague to understand. Describe how the requirements will be analyzed. Who will perform the analysis?

141. In case of software development; Should you have a test for each code module?

142. What are you counting on?

143. Do you really need to write this document at all?

144. Is requirements work dependent on any other specific Telecom Providers project or non-Telecom Providers project activities (e.g. funding, approvals, procurement)?

145. Do you understand the role that each stakeholder will play in the requirements process?

146. Define the help desk model. who will take full responsibility?

147. What information regarding the Telecom Providers project requirements will be reported?

148. Did you distinguish the scope of work the contractor(s) will be required to do?

149. Is infrastructure setup part of your Telecom Providers project?

150. How will requirements be managed?

151. Who is responsible for monitoring and tracking the Telecom Providers project requirements?

2.4 Requirements Documentation: Telecom Providers

152. How much does requirements engineering cost?

153. How will requirements be documented and who signs off on them?

154. Basic work/business process; high-level, what is being touched?

155. Who is involved?

156. What variations exist for a process?

157. If applicable; are there issues linked with the fact that this is an offshore Telecom Providers project?

158. What are current process problems?

159. Is new technology needed?

160. Have the benefits identified with the system being identified clearly?

161. What is a show stopper in the requirements?

162. What is the risk associated with cost and schedule?

163. How do you get the user to tell you what they want?

164. What happens when requirements are wrong?

165. Where do system and software requirements come from, what are sources?

166. How to document system requirements?

167. Who is interacting with the system?

168. Does your organization restrict technical alternatives?

169. How will the proposed Telecom Providers project help?

170. Is the requirement properly understood?

171. Completeness. are all functions required by the customer included?

2.5 Requirements Traceability Matrix: Telecom Providers

172. What are the chronologies, contingencies, consequences, criteria?

173. How small is small enough?

174. Is there a requirements traceability process in place?

175. Why do you manage scope?

176. Do you have a clear understanding of all subcontracts in place?

177. Why use a WBS?

178. Will you use a Requirements Traceability Matrix?

179. What is the WBS?

180. What percentage of Telecom Providers projects are producing traceability matrices between requirements and other work products?

181. Describe the process for approving requirements so they can be added to the traceability matrix and Telecom Providers project work can be performed. Will the Telecom Providers project requirements become approved in writing?

182. How do you manage scope?

183. How will it affect the stakeholders personally in career?

2.6 Project Scope Statement: Telecom Providers

184. Will the qa related information be reported regularly as part of the status reporting mechanisms?

185. Are there specific processes you will use to evaluate and approve/reject changes?

186. Does the scope statement still need some clarity?

187. Is the plan for Telecom Providers project resources adequate?

188. Is the quality function identified and assigned?

189. Elements of scope management that deal with concept development ?

190. Have you been able to easily identify success criteria and create objective measurements for each of the Telecom Providers project scopes goal statements?

191. Is the Telecom Providers project manager qualified and experienced in Telecom Providers project management?

192. What went right?

193. Risks?

194. Write a brief purpose statement for this Telecom

Providers project. Include a business justification statement. What is the product of this Telecom Providers project?

195. Is an issue management process documented and filed?

196. Is the plan for your organization of the Telecom Providers project resources adequate?

197. Is the change control process documented and on file?

198. Will you need a statement of work?

199. What actions will be taken to mitigate the risk?

200. If the scope changes, what will the impact be to your Telecom Providers project in terms of duration, cost, quality, or any other important areas of the Telecom Providers project?

201. Are there completion/verification criteria defined for each task producing an output?

2.7 Assumption and Constraint Log: Telecom Providers

202. What weaknesses do you have?

203. What to do at recovery?

204. What other teams / processes would be impacted by changes to the current process, and how?

205. Does the traceability documentation describe the tool and/or mechanism to be used to capture traceability throughout the life cycle?

206. How are new requirements or changes to requirements identified?

207. Is there a Steering Committee in place?

208. Does the Telecom Providers project have a formal Telecom Providers project Plan?

209. What does an audit system look like?

210. If appropriate, is the deliverable content consistent with current Telecom Providers project documents and in compliance with the Document Management Plan?

211. Are requirements management tracking tools and procedures in place?

212. Are best practices and metrics employed to

identify issues, progress, performance, etc.?

213. Does the document/deliverable meet all requirements (for example, statement of work) specific to this deliverable?

214. What do you log?

215. Are there processes defining how software will be developed including development methods, overall timeline for development, software product standards, and traceability?

216. Is the amount of effort justified by the anticipated value of forming a new process?

217. Is the process working, and people are not executing in compliance of the process?

218. Are processes for release management of new development from coding and unit testing, to integration testing, to training, and production defined and followed?

219. Violation trace: why ?

220. Does a documented Telecom Providers project organizational policy & plan (i.e. governance model) exist?

221. Is this model reasonable?

2.8 Work Breakdown Structure: Telecom Providers

222. Why would you develop a Work Breakdown Structure?

223. What is the probability that the Telecom Providers project duration will exceed xx weeks?

224. Where does it take place?

225. How much detail?

226. How will you and your Telecom Providers project team define the Telecom Providers projects scope and work breakdown structure?

227. What has to be done?

228. How big is a work-package?

229. When do you stop?

230. Can you make it?

231. When would you develop a Work Breakdown Structure?

232. Do you need another level?

233. Is it a change in scope?

234. What is the probability of completing the

Telecom Providers project in less that xx days?

235. When does it have to be done?

236. Why is it useful?

237. Is it still viable?

238. Who has to do it?

2.9 WBS Dictionary: Telecom Providers

239. Are significant decision points, constraints, and interfaces identified as key milestones?

240. Detailed schedules which support control account and work package start and completion dates/events?

241. Does the contractors system provide for the determination of cost variances attributable to the excess usage of material?

242. Is work properly classified as measured effort, LOE, or apportioned effort and appropriately separated?

243. Budgeted cost for work performed?

244. Are estimates developed by Telecom Providers project personnel coordinated with the already stated responsible for overall management to determine whether required resources will be available according to revised planning?

245. Is all budget available as management reserve identified and excluded from the performance measurement baseline?

246. Does the contractors system include procedures for measuring the performance of critical subcontractors?

247. Does the accounting system provide a basis for auditing records of direct costs chargeable to the contract?

248. Are direct or indirect cost adjustments being accomplished according to accounting procedures acceptable to us?

249. Are data being used by managers in an effective manner to ascertain Telecom Providers project or functional status, to identify reasons or significant variance, and to initiate appropriate corrective action?

250. Does the contractors system description or procedures require that the performance measurement baseline plus management reserve equal the contract budget base?

251. Identify potential or actual budget-based and time-based schedule variances?

252. The anticipated business volume?

253. Authorization to proceed with all authorized work?

254. What size should a work package be?

2.10 Schedule Management Plan: Telecom Providers

255. Are changes in deliverable commitments agreed to by all affected groups & individuals?

256. Is there any form of automated support for Issues Management?

257. Does a documented Telecom Providers project organizational policy & plan (i.e. governance model) exist?

258. Is there general agreement & acceptance of the current status and progress of the Telecom Providers project?

259. Are all vendor contracts closed out?

260. Are risk triggers captured?

261. Do Telecom Providers project managers participating in the Telecom Providers project know the Telecom Providers projects true status first hand?

262. Are tasks tracked by hours?

263. Has a quality assurance plan been developed for the Telecom Providers project?

264. Are the people assigned to the Telecom Providers project sufficiently qualified?

265. Staffing Requirements?

266. Are all payments made according to the contract(s)?

267. Will the Telecom Providers project sponsor be involved in preliminary schedule reviews?

268. Has the ims content been baselined and is it adequately controlled?

269. Have adequate resources been provided by management to ensure Telecom Providers project success?

270. What strengths do you have?

271. Are all attributes of the activities defined, including risk and uncertainty?

2.11 Activity List: Telecom Providers

272. How should ongoing costs be monitored to try to keep the Telecom Providers project within budget?

273. How difficult will it be to do specific activities on this Telecom Providers project?

274. How much slack is available in the Telecom Providers project?

275. What is your organizations history in doing similar activities?

276. What did not go as well?

277. How do you determine the late start (LS) for each activity?

278. When will the work be performed?

279. What will be performed?

280. What is the LF and LS for each activity?

281. The wbs is developed as part of a joint planning session. and how do you know that youhave done this right?

282. What is the total time required to complete the Telecom Providers project if no delays occur?

283. For other activities, how much delay can be tolerated?

284. How detailed should a Telecom Providers project get?

285. What is the probability the Telecom Providers project can be completed in xx weeks?

286. What went well?

287. Can you determine the activity that must finish, before this activity can start?

288. When do the individual activities need to start and finish?

289. Is infrastructure setup part of your Telecom Providers project?

2.12 Activity Attributes: Telecom Providers

290. How else could the items be grouped?

291. What is the general pattern here?

292. Activity: what is In the Bag?

293. How much activity detail is required?

294. How many days do you need to complete the work scope with a limit of X number of resources?

295. Which method produces the more accurate cost assignment?

296. How difficult will it be to complete specific activities on this Telecom Providers project?

297. Activity: fair or not fair?

298. Resources to accomplish the work?

299. Do you feel very comfortable with your prediction?

300. Can you re-assign any activities to another resource to resolve an over-allocation?

301. What is missing?

302. Are the required resources available?

303. How many resources do you need to complete the work scope within a limit of X number of days?

304. Does your organization of the data change its meaning?

305. What activity do you think you should spend the most time on?

306. How difficult will it be to do specific activities on this Telecom Providers project?

2.13 Milestone List: Telecom Providers

307. Continuity, supply chain robustness?

308. Describe the industry you are in and the market growth opportunities. What is the market for your technology, product or service?

309. How soon can the activity finish?

310. How will you get the word out to customers?

311. Own known vulnerabilities?

312. What has been done so far?

313. Identify critical paths (one or more) and which activities are on the critical path?

314. Describe your organizations strengths and core competencies. What factors will make your organization succeed?

315. Insurmountable weaknesses?

316. Global influences?

317. Competitive advantages?

318. Milestone pages should display the UserID of the person who added the milestone. Does a report or query exist that provides this audit information?

319. Which path is the critical path?

320. What are your competitors vulnerabilities?

321. Sustaining internal capabilities?

322. Timescales, deadlines and pressures?

323. Political effects?

324. Gaps in capabilities?

325. Effects on core activities, distraction?

2.14 Network Diagram: Telecom Providers

326. Exercise: what is the probability that the Telecom Providers project duration will exceed xx weeks?

327. What activity must be completed immediately before this activity can start?

328. What activities must follow this activity?

329. What to do and When?

330. What controls the start and finish of a job?

331. What job or jobs could run concurrently?

332. What are the tools?

333. Why must you schedule milestones, such as reviews, throughout the Telecom Providers project?

334. What can be done concurrently?

335. Will crashing x weeks return more in benefits than it costs?

336. What activities must occur simultaneously with this activity?

337. What job or jobs precede it?

338. What is the lowest cost to complete this Telecom

Providers project in xx weeks?

339. Planning: who, how long, what to do?

340. If the Telecom Providers project network diagram cannot change and you have extra personnel resources, what is the BEST thing to do?

341. Which type of network diagram allows you to depict four types of dependencies?

342. What job or jobs follow it?

343. What is the completion time?

2.15 Activity Resource Requirements: Telecom Providers

344. How many signatures do you require on a check and does this match what is in your policy and procedures?

345. Why do you do that?

346. How do you handle petty cash?

347. Do you use tools like decomposition and rolling-wave planning to produce the activity list and other outputs?

348. Which logical relationship does the PDM use most often?

349. Anything else?

350. When does monitoring begin?

351. Other support in specific areas?

352. What is the Work Plan Standard?

353. Organizational Applicability?

354. Is there anything planned that does not need to be here?

355. What are constraints that you might find during the Human Resource Planning process?

356. Are there unresolved issues that need to be addressed?

357. Time for overtime?

2.16 Resource Breakdown Structure: Telecom Providers

358. Which resource planning tool provides information on resource responsibility and accountability?

359. Who is allowed to see what data about which resources?

360. What is the primary purpose of the human resource plan?

361. When do they need the information?

362. What is Telecom Providers project communication management?

363. Changes based on input from stakeholders?

364. Who delivers the information?

365. Who is allowed to perform which functions?

366. Why is this important?

367. How should the information be delivered?

368. What is the purpose of assigning and documenting responsibility?

369. What can you do to improve productivity?

370. Why do you do it?

371. Which resources should be in the resource pool?

372. What defines a successful Telecom Providers project?

373. What are the requirements for resource data?

2.17 Activity Duration Estimates: Telecom Providers

374. Consider the examples of poor quality in information technology Telecom Providers projects presented in the What Went Wrong?

375. Do an internet search on earning pmp certification. be sure to search for yahoo groups related to this topic. what are the options you found to help people prepare for the exam?

376. Given your research into similar classes and the work you think is required for this Telecom Providers project, what assumptions, variables, or costs would you change from the information provided above?

377. Explanation notice how many choices are half right?

378. Research recruiting and retention strategies at three different companies. What distinguishes one organization from another in this area?

379. Does a process exist for approving or rejecting changes?

380. Account for the make-or-buy process and how to perform the financial calculations involved in the process. What are the main types of contracts if you do decide to outsource?

381. How can you use Microsoft Telecom Providers

project and Excel to assist in Telecom Providers project risk management?

382. Account for the four frames of organizations. How can they help Telecom Providers project managers understand your organizational context for Telecom Providers projects?

383. How do theories relate to Telecom Providers project management?

384. Do procedures exist that identify when and how human resources are introduced and removed from the Telecom Providers project?

385. Are procedures defined for calculating cost estimates?

386. How much time is required to develop it?

387. Are training needs identified when resources do not have the required skills to complete Telecom Providers project activities?

388. Who has the PRIMARY responsibility to solve this problem?

389. What are the main processes included in Telecom Providers project quality management?

390. Is training acquired to enhance the skills, knowledge and capabilities of the Telecom Providers project team?

391. What are the main parts of a scope statement?

392. What are the largest companies that provide information technology outsourcing services?

2.18 Duration Estimating Worksheet: Telecom Providers

393. Define the work as completely as possible. What work will be included in the Telecom Providers project?

394. Done before proceeding with this activity or what can be done concurrently?

395. Small or large Telecom Providers project?

396. Will the Telecom Providers project collaborate with the local community and leverage resources?

397. What work will be included in the Telecom Providers project?

398. Value pocket identification & quantification what are value pockets?

399. What is an Average Telecom Providers project?

400. Do any colleagues have experience with your organization and/or RFPs?

401. What utility impacts are there?

402. Can the Telecom Providers project be constructed as planned?

403. What info is needed?

404. Is a construction detail attached (to aid in explanation)?

405. When, then?

406. Does the Telecom Providers project provide innovative ways for stakeholders to overcome obstacles or deliver better outcomes?

407. When does your organization expect to be able to complete it?

408. What is next?

409. What is the total time required to complete the Telecom Providers project if no delays occur?

2.19 Project Schedule: Telecom Providers

410. What does that mean?

411. How can you address that situation?

412. To what degree is do you feel the entire team was committed to the Telecom Providers project schedule?

413. How do you know that youhave done this right?

414. Why do you need to manage Telecom Providers project Risk?

415. Verify that the update is accurate. Are all remaining durations correct?

416. What documents, if any, will the subcontractor provide (eg Telecom Providers project schedule, quality plan etc)?

417. How can you minimize or control changes to Telecom Providers project schedules?

418. How can slack be negative?

419. How many levels?

420. Master Telecom Providers project schedule?

421. Schedule/cost recovery?

422. Are quality inspections and review activities listed in the Telecom Providers project schedule(s)?

423. Did the final product meet or exceed user expectations?

424. Is there a Schedule Management Plan that establishes the criteria and activities for developing, monitoring and controlling the Telecom Providers project schedule?

425. Why is this particularly bad?

426. How can you fix it?

427. Is the structure for tracking the Telecom Providers project schedule well defined and assigned to a specific individual?

2.20 Cost Management Plan: Telecom Providers

428. Will the earned value reporting interface between time and cost management?

429. Is a stakeholder management plan in place that covers topics?

430. What would the life cycle costs be?

431. Environmental management – what changes in statutory environmental compliance requirements are anticipated during the Telecom Providers project?

432. Risk Analysis?

433. Technical and functional?

434. Has a capability assessment been conducted?

435. Does the Telecom Providers project have a formal Telecom Providers project Charter?

436. Escalation criteria met?

437. Are non-critical path items updated and agreed upon with the teams?

438. Are change requests logged and managed?

439. Similar Telecom Providers projects?

440. Are the quality tools and methods identified in the Quality Plan appropriate to the Telecom Providers project?

441. Are Telecom Providers project team members involved in detailed estimating and scheduling?

442. Is there an on-going process in place to monitor Telecom Providers project risks?

443. What would you do differently what did not work?

444. Is the assigned Telecom Providers project manager a PMP (Certified Telecom Providers project manager) and experienced?

445. Have key stakeholders been identified?

446. Is there a requirements change management processes in place?

2.21 Activity Cost Estimates: Telecom Providers

447. How do you fund change orders?

448. Vac -variance at completion, how much over/ under budget do you expect to be?

449. Specific - is the objective clear in terms of what, how, when, and where the situation will be changed?

450. Was it performed on time?

451. Performance bond should always provide what part of the contract value?

452. Can you change your activities?

453. What is a Telecom Providers project Management Plan?

454. What do you want to know about the stay to know if costs were inappropriately high or low?

455. What makes a good activity description?

456. How do you change activities?

457. What procedures are put in place regarding bidding and cost comparisons, if any?

458. Where can you get activity reports?

459. What communication items need improvement?

460. What are the audit requirements?

461. Does the activity serve a common type of customer?

462. Based on your Telecom Providers project communication management plan, what worked well?

463. Were decisions made in a timely manner?

464. Review – what are some common errors in activities to avoid?

465. What skill level is required to do the job?

2.22 Cost Estimating Worksheet: Telecom Providers

466. Is the Telecom Providers project responsive to community need?

467. What additional Telecom Providers project(s) could be initiated as a result of this Telecom Providers project?

468. Who is best positioned to know and assist in identifying corresponding factors?

469. How will the results be shared and to whom?

470. Will the Telecom Providers project collaborate with the local community and leverage resources?

471. What costs are to be estimated?

472. Is it feasible to establish a control group arrangement?

473. Can a trend be established from historical performance data on the selected measure and are the criteria for using trend analysis or forecasting methods met?

474. Identify the timeframe necessary to monitor progress and collect data to determine how the selected measure has changed?

475. Does the Telecom Providers project provide

innovative ways for stakeholders to overcome obstacles or deliver better outcomes?

476. What happens to any remaining funds not used?

477. What can be included?

478. What is the estimated labor cost today based upon this information?

479. What is the purpose of estimating?

480. Ask: are others positioned to know, are others credible, and will others cooperate?

481. What will others want?

2.23 Cost Baseline: Telecom Providers

482. Have the lessons learned been filed with the Telecom Providers project Management Office?

483. How likely is it to go wrong?

484. Has the Telecom Providers project (or Telecom Providers project phase) been evaluated against each objective established in the product description and Integrated Telecom Providers project Plan?

485. How accurate do cost estimates need to be?

486. What threats might prevent you from getting there?

487. What deliverables come first?

488. Have the resources used by the Telecom Providers project been reassigned to other units or Telecom Providers projects?

489. What is your organizations history in doing similar tasks?

490. Does it impact schedule, cost, quality?

491. What is it ?

492. Has training and knowledge transfer of the operations organization been completed?

493. When should cost estimates be developed?

494. Should a more thorough impact analysis be conducted?

495. Have the actual milestone completion dates been compared to the approved schedule?

496. Have all approved changes to the Telecom Providers project requirement been identified and impact on the performance, cost, and schedule baselines documented?

497. What is the reality?

498. If you sold 10x widgets on a day, what would the affect on profits be?

499. Does the suggested change request seem to represent a necessary enhancement to the product?

500. How do you manage cost?

501. Is the requested change request a result of changes in other Telecom Providers project(s)?

2.24 Quality Management Plan: Telecom Providers

502. Are there standards for code development?

503. How are calibration records kept?

504. What type of in-house testing do you conduct?

505. How are deviations from procedures handled?

506. How are people conducting sampling trained?

507. Does the plan conform to standards?

508. Does the program conduct field testing?

509. What are your organizations key processes (product, service, business, and support)?

510. What are the appropriate test methods to be used?

511. What are your organizations current levels and trends for the already stated measures related to employee wellbeing, satisfaction, and development?

512. Have all stakeholders been identified?

513. Is this a Requirement?

514. How do you document and correct nonconformances?

515. How is equipment calibrated?

516. Do you keep back-up copies of any data?

517. Do you periodically review your data quality system to see that it is up to date and appropriate?

518. Are there trends or hot spots?

519. Can the requirements be traced to the appropriate components of the solution, as well as test scripts?

520. Do trained quality assurance auditors conduct the audits as defined in the Quality Management Plan and scheduled by the Telecom Providers project manager?

521. How does your organization perform analyzes to assess overall organizational performance and set priorities?

2.25 Quality Metrics: Telecom Providers

522. Why is now the time for quality metrics?

523. What group is empowered to define quality requirements?

524. Which report did you use to create the data you are submitting?

525. What method of measurement do you use?

526. Were number of defects identified?

527. How do you calculate corresponding metrics?

528. What do you measure?

529. What is the benchmark?

530. Have alternatives been defined in the event that failure occurs?

531. When will the Final Guidance will be issued?

532. Who is willing to lead?

533. Was review conducted per standard protocols?

534. There are many reasons to shore up quality-related metrics, and what metrics are important?

535. What can manufacturing professionals do to ensure quality is seen as an integral part of the entire product lifecycle?

536. How is it being measured?

537. What metrics do you measure?

538. Are interface issues coordinated?

539. What does this tell us?

540. Which data do others need in one place to target areas of improvement?

541. How do you know if everyone is trying to improve the right things?

2.26 Process Improvement Plan: Telecom Providers

542. Purpose of goal: the motive is determined by asking, why do you want to achieve this goal?

543. Have storage and access mechanisms and procedures been determined?

544. Has the time line required to move measurement results from the points of collection to databases or users been established?

545. Does explicit definition of the measures exist?

546. How do you measure?

547. What personnel are the coaches for your initiative?

548. Have the supporting tools been developed or acquired?

549. Who should prepare the process improvement action plan?

550. What is the return on investment?

551. How do you manage quality?

552. If a process improvement framework is being used, which elements will help the problems and goals listed?

553. Modeling current processes is great, and will you ever see a return on that investment?

554. Are you making progress on the goals?

555. What lessons have you learned so far?

556. Where do you want to be?

557. What personnel are the champions for the initiative?

558. The motive is determined by asking, Why do you want to achieve this goal?

559. Everyone agrees on what process improvement is, right?

560. To elicit goal statements, do you ask a question such as, What do you want to achieve?

2.27 Responsibility Assignment Matrix: Telecom Providers

561. Are others working on the right things?

562. Does each activity-deliverable have exactly one Accountable responsibility, so that accountability is clear and decisions can be made quickly?

563. What cost control tool do many experts say is crucial to Telecom Providers project management?

564. Are data elements reconcilable between internal summary reports and reports forwarded to stakeholders?

565. How do you manage human resources?

566. Where does all this information come from?

567. Does the contractors system provide unit or lot costs when applicable?

568. Does the contractors system identify work accomplishment against the schedule plan?

569. What does wbs accomplish?

570. How many people do you need?

571. Is the anticipated (firm and potential) business base Telecom Providers projected in a rational, consistent manner?

572. What materials and procurements needed?

573. Do others have the time to dedicate to your Telecom Providers project?

574. Are work packages assigned to performing organizations?

575. Undistributed budgets, if any?

576. Contemplated overhead expenditure for each period based on the best information currently available?

577. Too many is: do all the identified roles need to be routinely informed or only in exceptional circumstances?

578. Are meaningful indicators identified for use in measuring the status of cost and schedule performance?

579. Are the overhead pools formally and adequately identified?

2.28 Roles and Responsibilities: Telecom Providers

580. Who: who is involved?

581. Are your budgets supportive of a culture of quality data?

582. Does your vision/mission support a culture of quality data?

583. What should you do now to prepare for your career 5+ years from now?

584. What expectations were NOT met?

585. Authority: what areas/Telecom Providers projects in your work do you have the authority to decide upon and act on the already stated decisions?

586. Who is responsible for implementation activities and where will the functions, roles and responsibilities be defined?

587. Do you take the time to clearly define roles and responsibilities on Telecom Providers project tasks?

588. Accountabilities: what are the roles and responsibilities of individual team members?

589. What expectations were met?

590. Is the data complete?

591. What is working well?

592. Once the responsibilities are defined for the Telecom Providers project, have the deliverables, roles and responsibilities been clearly communicated to every participant?

593. How is your work-life balance?

594. What are your major roles and responsibilities in the area of performance measurement and assessment?

595. Are Telecom Providers project team roles and responsibilities identified and documented?

596. To decide whether to use a quality measurement, ask how will you know when it is achieved?

597. Once the responsibilities are defined for the Telecom Providers project, have the deliverables, roles and responsibilities been clearly communicated to every participant?

598. Influence: what areas of organizational decision making are you able to influence when you do not have authority to make the final decision?

599. What should you do now to ensure that you are meeting all expectations of your current position?

2.29 Human Resource Management Plan: Telecom Providers

600. Who will be impacted (both positively and negatively) as a result of or during the execution of this Telecom Providers project?

601. Is a payment system in place with proper reviews and approvals?

602. Timeline and milestones?

603. Are staff skills known and available for each task?

604. Was the Telecom Providers project schedule reviewed by all stakeholders and formally accepted?

605. Are metrics used to evaluate and manage Vendors?

606. Are quality metrics defined?

607. Are post milestone Telecom Providers project reviews (PMPR) conducted with your organization at least once a year?

608. Are procurement deliverables arriving on time and to specification?

609. Who is evaluated?

610. What were things that you did very well and want to do the same again on the next Telecom Providers

project?

611. Were stakeholders aware and supportive of the principles and practices of modern cost estimation?

612. Were Telecom Providers project team members involved in the development of activity & task decomposition?

613. List the assumptions made to date. What did you have to assume to be true to complete the charter?

614. Have stakeholder accountabilities & responsibilities been clearly defined?

615. Based on your Telecom Providers project communication management plan, what worked well?

616. Are mitigation strategies identified?

617. Is Telecom Providers project status reviewed with the steering and executive teams at appropriate intervals?

618. Is there a set of procedures to capture, analyze and act on quality metrics?

2.30 Communications Management Plan: Telecom Providers

619. What to learn?

620. Are others needed?

621. Who needs to know and how much?

622. Who did you turn to if you had questions?

623. Is the stakeholder role recognized by your organization?

624. Do you then often overlook a key stakeholder or stakeholder group?

625. How were corresponding initiatives successful?

626. Who to share with?

627. Will messages be directly related to the release strategy or phases of the Telecom Providers project?

628. Which stakeholders are thought leaders, influences, or early adopters?

629. Who to learn from?

630. What is the stakeholders level of authority?

631. Which team member will work with each stakeholder?

632. What data is going to be required?

633. Who is the stakeholder?

634. What is the political influence?

635. How did the term stakeholder originate?

636. How do you manage communications?

637. Are you constantly rushing from meeting to meeting?

2.31 Risk Management Plan: Telecom Providers

638. Does the customer have a solid idea of what is required?

639. Is the customer technically sophisticated in the product area?

640. Are the software tools integrated with each other?

641. Is security a central objective?

642. Does the customer understand the software process?

643. Is Telecom Providers project scope stable?

644. Litigation – what is the probability that lawsuits will cause problems or delays in the Telecom Providers project?

645. Why do you want risk management?

646. What is the probability the risk avoidance strategy will be successful?

647. Who/what can assist?

648. What should be done with non-critical risks?

649. Was an original risk assessment/risk management

plan completed?

650. Do you train all developers in the process?

651. My Telecom Providers project leader has suddenly left your organization, what do you do?

652. What is the likelihood that your organization would accept responsibility for the risk?

653. Are team members trained in the use of the tools?

654. Why do you need to manage Telecom Providers project Risk?

655. How is the audit profession changing?

656. How is risk identification performed?

657. How is risk monitoring performed?

2.32 Risk Register: Telecom Providers

658. Who needs to know about this?

659. What are you going to do to limit the Telecom Providers projects risk exposure due to the identified risks?

660. Are your objectives at risk?

661. Severity Prediction?

662. Market risk -will the new service or product be useful to your organization or marketable to others?

663. Risk probability and impact: how will the probabilities and impacts of risk items be assessed?

664. What has changed since the last period?

665. Have other controls and solutions been implemented in other services which could be applied as an alternative to additional funding?

666. People risk -are people with appropriate skills available to help complete the Telecom Providers project?

667. Cost/benefit – how much will the proposed mitigations cost and how does this cost compare with the potential cost of the risk event/situation should it occur?

668. What should you do when?

669. What is the appropriate level of risk management for this Telecom Providers project?

670. Are corrective measures implemented as planned?

671. Having taken action, how did the responses effect change, and where is the Telecom Providers project now?

672. What could prevent you delivering on the strategic program objectives and what is being done to mitigate corresponding issues?

673. When is it going to be done?

674. Are implemented controls working as others should?

675. Which key risks have ineffective responses or outstanding improvement actions?

676. What further options might be available for responding to the risk?

677. What is the probability and impact of the risk occurring?

2.33 Probability and Impact Assessment: Telecom Providers

678. Are requirements fully understood by the software engineering team and customers?

679. What will be the impact or consequence if the risk occurs?

680. Risk categorization -which of your categories has more risk than others?

681. What kind of preparation would be required to do this?

682. Monitoring of the overall Telecom Providers project status – are there any changes in the Telecom Providers project that can effect and cause new possible risks?

683. How do the products attain the specifications?

684. Can you stabilize dynamic risk factors?

685. Is the customer willing to participate in reviews?

686. What are the tools and techniques used in managing the challenges faced?

687. How completely has the customer been identified?

688. Have you ascribed a level of confidence to every

critical technical objective?

689. How do risks change during the Telecom Providers projects life cycle?

690. What should be the level of coordination?

691. Are enough people available?

692. What are the channels available for distribution to the customer?

693. Risk urgency assessment -which of your risks could occur soon, or require a longer planning time?

694. What is the impact if the risk does occur?

695. Have you worked with the customer in the past?

696. Are flexibility and reuse paramount?

697. What should be the external organizations responsibility vis-à-vis total stake in the Telecom Providers project?

2.34 Probability and Impact Matrix: Telecom Providers

698. What can you do about it?

699. What can you use the analyzed risks for?

700. How to prioritize risks?

701. Should the risk be taken at all?

702. What should be the gestation period for the Telecom Providers project with this technology?

703. How are the local factors going to affect the absorption?

704. Is the customer willing to establish rapid communication links with the developer?

705. What should be done with risks on the watch list?

706. Why do you need to manage Telecom Providers project Risk?

707. Which role do you have in the Telecom Providers project?

708. Who are the owners?

709. What will the damage be?

710. What is the likelihood?

711. What are the current requirements of the customer?

712. What are ways to measure and evaluate risks?

713. What is the level of experience available with your organization?

714. What has the Telecom Providers project manager forgotten to do?

2.35 Risk Data Sheet: Telecom Providers

715. What can you do?

716. What is the likelihood of it happening?

717. Are new hazards created?

718. What are you trying to achieve (Objectives)?

719. What actions can be taken to eliminate or remove risk?

720. How reliable is the data source?

721. Type of risk identified?

722. Is the data sufficiently specified in terms of the type of failure being analyzed, and its frequency or probability?

723. What were the Causes that contributed?

724. Has the most cost-effective solution been chosen?

725. Potential for recurrence?

726. What are your core values?

727. Do effective diagnostic tests exist?

728. What are the main threats to your existence?

729. What are you weak at and therefore need to do better?

730. What if client refuses?

731. What are you here for (Mission)?

732. What will be the consequences if it happens?

2.36 Procurement Management Plan: Telecom Providers

733. Does a documented Telecom Providers project organizational policy & plan (i.e. governance model) exist?

734. Have adequate resources been provided by management to ensure Telecom Providers project success?

735. How long will it take for the purchase cost to be the same as the lease cost?

736. Is there an issues management plan in place?

737. Does the Telecom Providers project have a Quality Culture?

738. Are governance roles and responsibilities documented?

739. Are the Telecom Providers project team members located locally to the users/stakeholders?

740. Has a Telecom Providers project Communications Plan been developed?

741. Is Telecom Providers project work proceeding in accordance with the original Telecom Providers project schedule?

742. Is a pmo (Telecom Providers project

management office) in place which provides oversight to the Telecom Providers project?

743. Has the scope management document been updated and distributed to help prevent scope creep?

744. Is there a formal process for updating the Telecom Providers project baseline?

745. Are changes in scope (deliverable commitments) agreed to by all affected groups & individuals?

746. Are quality inspections and review activities listed in the Telecom Providers project schedule(s)?

747. Is there a procurement management plan in place?

748. Is quality monitored from the perspective of the customers needs and expectations?

749. Are decisions captured in a decisions log?

2.37 Source Selection Criteria: Telecom Providers

750. Will the technical evaluation factor unnecessarily force the acquisition into a higher-priced market segment?

751. Are evaluators ready to begin this task?

752. What should be considered when developing evaluation standards?

753. In which phase of the acquisition process cycle does source qualifications reside?

754. What is price analysis and when should it be performed?

755. What is the effect of the debriefing schedule on potential protests?

756. How will you evaluate offerors proposals?

757. Are responses to considerations adequate?

758. Can you prevent comparison of proposals?

759. How is past performance evaluated?

760. Do you prepare an independent cost estimate?

761. Are types/quantities of material, facilities appropriate?

762. Does an evaluation need to include the identification of strengths and weaknesses?

763. When is it appropriate to issue a DRFP?

764. How important is cost in the source selection decision relative to past performance and technical considerations?

765. How should oral presentations be evaluated?

766. What information may not be provided?

767. Do you have a plan to document consensus results including disposition of any disagreement by individual evaluators?

768. Can you reasonably estimate total organization requirements for the coming year?

769. Do you consider all weaknesses, significant weaknesses, and deficiencies?

2.38 Stakeholder Management Plan: Telecom Providers

770. Is pert / critical path or equivalent methodology being used?

771. Is documentation created for communication with the suppliers and vendors?

772. Why would a customer be interested in a particular product or service?

773. Does the system design reflect the requirements?

774. Are the quality tools and methods identified in the Quality Plan appropriate to the Telecom Providers project?

775. Were Telecom Providers project team members involved in detailed estimating and scheduling?

776. What are reporting requirements?

777. Who will be responsible for managing and maintaining the Issues Register?

778. Are estimating assumptions and constraints captured?

779. Are milestone deliverables effectively tracked and compared to Telecom Providers project plan?

780. Has a structured approach been used to break

work effort into manageable components (WBS)?

781. Describe the process that will be used to design, develop, review, accept, distribute and change outputs. Will all outputs delivered by the Telecom Providers project follow the same process?

2.39 Change Management Plan: Telecom Providers

782. Who might be able to help you the most?

783. Is there an adequate supply of people for the new roles?

784. How do you gain sponsors buy-in to the communication plan?

785. How much change management is needed?

786. What time commitment will this involve?

787. Do you need new systems?

788. What is the most positive interpretation it can receive?

789. What are the essentials of the message?

790. Who will be the change levers?

791. Is there a software application relevant to this deliverable?

792. What new behaviours are required?

793. What are the training strategies?

794. How far reaching in your organization is the change?

795. Are there any restrictions on who can receive the communications?

796. Has an information & communications plan been developed?

797. What relationships will change?

798. Where will the funds come from?

799. Do you need a new organization structure?

3.0 Executing Process Group: Telecom Providers

800. Do schedule issues conflicts?

801. Is the Telecom Providers project performing better or worse than planned?

802. Could a new application negatively affect the current IT infrastructure?

803. What are some crucial elements of a good Telecom Providers project plan?

804. How will professionals learn what is expected from them what the deliverables are?

805. Will new hardware or software be required for servers or client machines?

806. Just how important is your work to the overall success of the Telecom Providers project?

807. How many different communication channels does the Telecom Providers project team have?

808. Is the schedule for the set products being met?

809. When do you share the scorecard with managers?

810. What is the shortest possible time it will take to complete this Telecom Providers project?

811. What areas does the group agree are the biggest success on the Telecom Providers project?

812. Will a new application be developed using existing hardware, software, and networks?

813. When will the Telecom Providers project be done?

814. What are the main types of goods and services being outsourced?

815. What is the critical path for this Telecom Providers project and how long is it?

816. What were things that you did well, and could improve, and how?

817. How do you prevent staff are just doing busywork to pass the time?

818. Will outside resources be needed to help?

3.1 Team Member Status Report: Telecom Providers

819. What is to be done?

820. Is there evidence that staff is taking a more professional approach toward management of your organizations Telecom Providers projects?

821. Why is it to be done?

822. The problem with Reward & Recognition Programs is that the truly deserving people all too often get left out. How can you make it practical?

823. Are the attitudes of staff regarding Telecom Providers project work improving?

824. Do you have an Enterprise Telecom Providers project Management Office (EPMO)?

825. How can you make it practical?

826. Does your organization have the means (staff, money, contract, etc.) to produce or to acquire the product, good, or service?

827. How it is to be done?

828. Does every department have to have a Telecom Providers project Manager on staff?

829. How does this product, good, or service meet

the needs of the Telecom Providers project and your organization as a whole?

830. When a teams productivity and success depend on collaboration and the efficient flow of information, what generally fails them?

831. What specific interest groups do you have in place?

832. How much risk is involved?

833. Are your organizations Telecom Providers projects more successful over time?

834. How will resource planning be done?

835. Does the product, good, or service already exist within your organization?

836. Are the products of your organizations Telecom Providers projects meeting customers objectives?

837. Will the staff do training or is that done by a third party?

3.2 Change Request: Telecom Providers

838. Where do changes come from?

839. What can be filed?

840. What is a Change Request Form?

841. What are the Impacts to your organization?

842. What should be regulated in a change control operating instruction?

843. Who can suggest changes?

844. Who is responsible to authorize changes?

845. How does your organization control changes before and after software is released to a customer?

846. How can changes be graded?

847. Are there requirements attributes that are strongly related to the occurrence of defects and failures?

848. How to get changes (code) out in a timely manner?

849. Who needs to approve change requests?

850. Will all change requests be unconditionally

tracked through this process?

851. Will there be a change request form in use?

852. Who is included in the change control team?

853. Has your address changed?

854. How do team members communicate with each other?

855. Describe how modifications, enhancements, defects and/or deficiencies shall be notified (e.g. Problem Reports, Change Requests etc) and managed. Detail warranty and/or maintenance periods?

856. How many lines of code must be changed to implement the change?

3.3 Change Log: Telecom Providers

857. When was the request submitted?

858. Is this a mandatory replacement?

859. When was the request approved?

860. Is the change backward compatible without limitations?

861. Is the requested change request a result of changes in other Telecom Providers project(s)?

862. Will the Telecom Providers project fail if the change request is not executed?

863. How does this change affect scope?

864. Who initiated the change request?

865. Is the change request open, closed or pending?

866. Do the described changes impact on the integrity or security of the system?

867. Is the submitted change a new change or a modification of a previously approved change?

868. How does this change affect the timeline of the schedule?

869. Is the change request within Telecom Providers project scope?

870. How does this relate to the standards developed for specific business processes?

871. Does the suggested change request represent a desired enhancement to the products functionality?

3.4 Decision Log: Telecom Providers

872. What alternatives/risks were considered?

873. Behaviors; what are guidelines that the team has identified that will assist them with getting the most out of team meetings?

874. What makes you different or better than others companies selling the same thing?

875. What was the rationale for the decision?

876. What eDiscovery problem or issue did your organization set out to fix or make better?

877. Who is the decisionmaker?

878. How do you know when you are achieving it?

879. How consolidated and comprehensive a story can you tell by capturing currently available incident data in a central location and through a log of key decisions during an incident?

880. What is your overall strategy for quality control / quality assurance procedures?

881. Adversarial environment. is your opponent open to a non-traditional workflow, or will it likely challenge anything you do?

882. Meeting purpose; why does this team meet?

883. How does the use a Decision Support System influence the strategies/tactics or costs?

884. How does an increasing emphasis on cost containment influence the strategies and tactics used?

885. Do strategies and tactics aimed at less than full control reduce the costs of management or simply shift the cost burden?

886. At what point in time does loss become unacceptable?

887. Is your opponent open to a non-traditional workflow, or will it likely challenge anything you do?

888. How does provision of information, both in terms of content and presentation, influence acceptance of alternative strategies?

889. Decision-making process; how will the team make decisions?

890. With whom was the decision shared or considered?

891. Does anything need to be adjusted?

3.5 Quality Audit: Telecom Providers

892. Does the report read coherently?

893. Is your organizational structure established and each positions responsibility defined?

894. What experience do staff have in the type of work that the audit entails?

895. Are all complaints involving the possible failure of a device, labeling, or packaging to meet any of its specifications reviewed, evaluated, and investigated?

896. How does your organization know that its system for examining work done is appropriately effective and constructive?

897. How does your organization know that its system for inducting new staff to maximize workplace contributions are appropriately effective and constructive?

898. How does your organization know that its promotions system is appropriately effective, constructive and fair?

899. If your organization thinks it is doing something well, can it prove this?

900. How does your organization know that its relationships with the community at large are appropriately effective and constructive?

901. Have personnel cleanliness and health requirements been established?

902. How does your organization know that its staff entrance standards are appropriately effective and constructive and being implemented consistently?

903. How does your organization know whether they are adhering to mission and achieving objectives?

904. How does your organization know that its risk management system is appropriately effective and constructive?

905. Does the audit organization have experience in performing the required work for entities of your type and size?

906. For each device to be reconditioned, are device specifications, such as appropriate engineering drawings, component specifications and software specifications, maintained?

907. Are the intentions consistent with external obligations (such as applicable laws)?

908. How does your organization know that its system for supporting staff research capability is appropriately effective and constructive?

909. How does your organization know that the research supervision provided to its staff is appropriately effective and constructive?

910. How does your organization know that the system for managing its facilities is appropriately

effective and constructive?

911. How is the Strategic Plan (and other plans) reviewed and revised?

3.6 Team Directory: Telecom Providers

912. Process decisions: which organizational elements and which individuals will be assigned management functions?

913. How will the team handle changes?

914. Who will write the meeting minutes and distribute?

915. Timing: when do the effects of communication take place?

916. What are you going to deliver or accomplish?

917. What needs to be communicated?

918. Who are the Team Members?

919. Who should receive information (all stakeholders)?

920. How and in what format should information be presented?

921. Where should the information be distributed?

922. Where will the product be used and/or delivered or built when appropriate?

923. Does a Telecom Providers project team directory list all resources assigned to the Telecom Providers project?

924. How does the team resolve conflicts and ensure tasks are completed?

925. Process decisions: are all start-up, turn over and close out requirements of the contract satisfied?

926. Decisions: what could be done better to improve the quality of the constructed product?

927. Process decisions: are there any statutory or regulatory issues relevant to the timely execution of work?

928. Who will be the stakeholders on your next Telecom Providers project?

929. When does information need to be distributed?

3.7 Team Operating Agreement: Telecom Providers

930. How will you resolve conflict efficiently and respectfully?

931. Methodologies: how will key team processes be implemented, such as training, research, work deliverable production, review and approval processes, knowledge management, and meeting procedures?

932. Do team members reside in more than two countries?

933. Do you determine the meeting length and time of day?

934. The method to be used in the decision making process; Will it be consensus, majority rule, or the supervisor having the final say?

935. Are team roles clearly defined and accepted?

936. How does teaming fit in with overall organizational goals and meet organizational needs?

937. Do you solicit member feedback about meetings and what would make them better?

938. Do you record meetings for the already stated unable to attend?

939. What resources can be provided for the team in terms of equipment, space, time for training, protected time and space for meetings, and travel allowances?

940. Did you determine the technology methods that best match the messages to be communicated?

941. Did you delegate tasks such as taking meeting minutes, presenting a topic and soliciting input?

942. Do you listen for voice tone and word choice to understand the meaning behind words?

943. How will your group handle planned absences?

944. Must your members collaborate successfully to complete Telecom Providers projects?

945. Does your team need access to all documents and information at all times?

946. How do you want to be thought of and known within your organization?

947. Do you brief absent members after they view meeting notes or listen to a recording?

948. What types of accommodations will be formulated and put in place for sustaining the team?

949. Conflict resolution: how will disputes and other conflicts be mediated or resolved?

3.8 Team Performance Assessment: Telecom Providers

950. To what degree will the team ensure that all members equitably share the work essential to the success of the team?

951. Where to from here?

952. Lack of method variance in self-reported affect and perceptions at work: Reality or artifact?

953. To what degree do team members understand one anothers roles and skills?

954. To what degree can the team measure progress against specific goals?

955. To what degree do team members feel that the purpose of the team is important, if not exciting?

956. Is there a particular method of data analysis that you would recommend as a means of demonstrating that method variance is not of great concern for a given dataset?

957. To what degree will new and supplemental skills be introduced as the need is recognized?

958. To what degree are the goals ambitious?

959. To what degree does the teams purpose contain themes that are particularly meaningful and

memorable?

960. What are you doing specifically to develop the leaders around you?

961. How do you keep key people outside the group informed about its accomplishments?

962. To what degree are the skill areas critical to team performance present?

963. If you have criticized someones work for method variance in your role as reviewer, what was the circumstance?

964. Delaying market entry: how long is too long?

965. To what degree are staff involved as partners in the improvement process?

966. To what degree are corresponding categories of skills either actually or potentially represented across the membership?

967. Can familiarity breed backup?

968. What makes opportunities more or less obvious?

969. To what degree will the team adopt a concrete, clearly understood, and agreed-upon approach that will result in achievement of the teams goals?

3.9 Team Member Performance Assessment: Telecom Providers

970. What happens if a team member receives a Rating of Unsatisfactory?

971. What future plans (e.g., modifications) do you have for your program?

972. What tools are available to determine whether all contract functional and compliance areas of performance objectives, measures, and incentives have been met?

973. What are acceptable governance changes?

974. What were the challenges that resulted for training and assessment?

975. To what degree are the goals realistic?

976. To what degree can team members meet frequently enough to accomplish the teams ends?

977. What are best practices in use for the performance measurement system?

978. What evaluation results do you have?

979. Is there reluctance to join a team?

980. To what degree can all members engage in open and interactive considerations?

981. Verify business objectives. Are they appropriate, and well-articulated?

982. What is the Business Management Oversight Process?

983. How do you determine which data are the most important to use, analyze, or review?

984. How do you start collaborating?

985. Does the rater (supervisor) have the authority or responsibility to tell an employee that the employees performance is unsatisfactory?

986. To what degree do team members frequently explore the teams purpose and its implications?

987. What stakeholders must be involved in the development and oversight of the performance plan?

988. What are the standards or expectations for success?

989. Does statute or regulation require the job responsibility?

3.10 Issue Log: Telecom Providers

990. What would have to change?

991. In classifying stakeholders, which approach to do so are you using?

992. What is the impact on the Business Case?

993. Who do you turn to if you have questions?

994. Who reported the issue?

995. What is the status of the issue?

996. What steps can you take for positive relationships?

997. What date was the issue resolved?

998. Is there an important stakeholder who is actively opposed and will not receive messages?

999. Who were proponents/opponents?

1000. Are there too many who have an interest in some aspect of your work?

1001. Do you feel more overwhelmed by stakeholders?

1002. What effort will a change need?

1003. How is this initiative related to other portfolios,

programs, or Telecom Providers projects?

1004. Why do you manage communications?

1005. Who is the issue assigned to?

1006. What are the typical contents?

1007. Which stakeholders can influence others?

4.0 Monitoring and Controlling Process Group: Telecom Providers

1008. Were sponsors and decision makers available when needed outside regularly scheduled meetings?

1009. How well did the chosen processes fit the needs of the Telecom Providers project?

1010. How were collaborations developed, and how are they sustained?

1011. Feasibility: how much money, time, and effort can you put into this?

1012. What are the goals of the program?

1013. Key stakeholders to work with. How many potential communications channels exist on the Telecom Providers project?

1014. How to ensure validity, quality and consistency?

1015. Have operating capacities been created and/or reinforced in partners?

1016. How well did you do?

1017. What is the expected monetary value of the Telecom Providers project?

1018. How is agile Telecom Providers project management done?

1019. What were things that you need to improve?

1020. Do the partners have sufficient financial capacity to keep up the benefits produced by the programme?

1021. Is the program making progress in helping to achieve the set results?

1022. Is there undesirable impact on staff or resources?

1023. Who needs to be engaged upfront to ensure use of results?

1024. Do the products created live up to the necessary quality?

1025. Is there sufficient funding available for this?

4.1 Project Performance Report: Telecom Providers

1026. To what degree can the team ensure that all members are individually and jointly accountable for the teams purpose, goals, approach, and work-products?

1027. To what degree does the formal organization make use of individual resources and meet individual needs?

1028. How can Telecom Providers project sustainability be maintained?

1029. To what degree does the information network provide individuals with the information they require?

1030. What is in it for you?

1031. What is the degree to which rules govern information exchange between groups?

1032. To what degree does the task meet individual needs?

1033. To what degree are the demands of the task compatible with and converge with the relationships of the informal organization?

1034. To what degree will the approach capitalize on and enhance the skills of all team members in a manner that takes into consideration other demands on members of the team?

1035. To what degree are the tasks requirements reflected in the flow and storage of information?

1036. To what degree do members articulate the goals beyond the team membership?

1037. To what degree are the demands of the task compatible with and converge with the mission and functions of the formal organization?

1038. To what degree can team members frequently and easily communicate with one another?

1039. To what degree do the goals specify concrete team work products?

1040. To what degree do individual skills and abilities match task demands?

1041. To what degree are the teams goals and objectives clear, simple, and measurable?

4.2 Variance Analysis: Telecom Providers

1042. Are management actions taken to reduce indirect costs when there are significant adverse variances?

1043. Are all authorized tasks assigned to identified organizational elements?

1044. Are records maintained to show how undistributed budgets are controlled?

1045. What costs are avoidable if one or more customers are dropped?

1046. Why are standard cost systems used?

1047. Is there a logical explanation for any variance?

1048. Are there changes in the direct base to which overhead costs are allocated?

1049. What is the expected future profitability of each customer?

1050. Who is generally responsible for monitoring and taking action on variances?

1051. Are procedures for variance analysis documented and consistently applied at the control account level and selected WBS and organizational levels at least monthly as a routine task?

1052. Are there knowledgeable Telecom Providers projections of future performance?

1053. Are estimates of costs at completion generated in a rational, consistent manner?

1054. How does your organization allocate the cost of shared expenses and services?

1055. There are detailed schedules which support control account and work package start and completion dates/events?

1056. Favorable or unfavorable variance?

1057. Is the anticipated (firm and potential) business base Telecom Providers projected in a rational, consistent manner?

1058. What does a favorable labor efficiency variance mean?

4.3 Earned Value Status: Telecom Providers

1059. Earned value can be used in almost any Telecom Providers project situation and in almost any Telecom Providers project environment. it may be used on large Telecom Providers projects, medium sized Telecom Providers projects, tiny Telecom Providers projects (in cut-down form), complex and simple Telecom Providers projects and in any market sector. some people, of course, know all about earned value, they have used it for years - but perhaps not as effectively as they could have?

1060. Validation is a process of ensuring that the developed system will actually achieve the stakeholders desired outcomes; Are you building the right product? What do you validate?

1061. Where is evidence-based earned value in your organization reported?

1062. Are you hitting your Telecom Providers projects targets?

1063. What is the unit of forecast value?

1064. How much is it going to cost by the finish?

1065. Verification is a process of ensuring that the developed system satisfies the stakeholders agreements and specifications; Are you building the product right? What do you verify?

1066. Where are your problem areas?

1067. When is it going to finish?

1068. How does this compare with other Telecom Providers projects?

1069. If earned value management (EVM) is so good in determining the true status of a Telecom Providers project and Telecom Providers project its completion, why is it that hardly any one uses it in information systems related Telecom Providers projects?

4.4 Risk Audit: Telecom Providers

1070. Does your organization communicate regularly and effectively with its members?

1071. Are staff committed for the duration of the product?

1072. If applicable; does the software interface with new or unproven hardware or unproven vendor products?

1073. Are your rules, by-laws and practices non-discriminatory?

1074. Do requirements put excessive performance constraints on the product?

1075. Do you have a procedure for dealing with complaints?

1076. Do staff understand the extent of duty of care?

1077. From an empirical perspective, does the business risk approach lead to a more effective audit, or simply to increased consulting revenue detrimental to audit rigor?

1078. Will participants be required to sign a legally counselled waiver or risk disclaimer when entering an event?

1079. What are the outcomes you are looking for?

1080. Do requirements demand the use of new analysis, design, or testing methods?

1081. What resources are needed to achieve program results?

1082. Does your organization have a social media policy and procedure?

1083. What risk does not having unique identification present?

1084. Are corresponding safety and risk management policies posted for all to see?

1085. Where will the next scandal or adverse media involving your organization come from?

1086. What are the differences and similarities between strategic and operational risks in your organization?

1087. Are there any forms the staff is required to sign?

1088. Should additional substantive testing be conducted because of the risk audit results?

1089. What compliance systems do you have in place to address quality, errors, and outcomes?

4.5 Contractor Status Report: Telecom Providers

1090. What are the minimum and optimal bandwidth requirements for the proposed solution?

1091. Are there contractual transfer concerns?

1092. Who can list a Telecom Providers project as organization experience, your organization or a previous employee of your organization?

1093. What was the overall budget or estimated cost?

1094. If applicable; describe your standard schedule for new software version releases. Are new software version releases included in the standard maintenance plan?

1095. What process manages the contracts?

1096. What is the average response time for answering a support call?

1097. What was the budget or estimated cost for your organizations services?

1098. What was the actual budget or estimated cost for your organizations services?

1099. Describe how often regular updates are made to the proposed solution. Are corresponding regular updates included in the standard maintenance plan?

1100. How is risk transferred?

1101. What was the final actual cost?

1102. How does the proposed individual meet each requirement?

1103. How long have you been using the services?

4.6 Formal Acceptance: Telecom Providers

1104. Did the Telecom Providers project achieve its MOV?

1105. What was done right?

1106. What lessons were learned about your Telecom Providers project management methodology?

1107. Was the Telecom Providers project goal achieved?

1108. Does it do what client said it would?

1109. How does your team plan to obtain formal acceptance on your Telecom Providers project?

1110. Who supplies data?

1111. What can you do better next time?

1112. What function(s) does it fill or meet?

1113. Does it do what Telecom Providers project team said it would?

1114. Did the Telecom Providers project manager and team act in a professional and ethical manner?

1115. Do you buy pre-configured systems or build your own configuration?

1116. Who would use it?

1117. Was the sponsor/customer satisfied?

1118. Was the Telecom Providers project work done on time, within budget, and according to specification?

1119. What is the Acceptance Management Process?

1120. Was the Telecom Providers project managed well?

1121. What are the requirements against which to test, Who will execute?

1122. Is formal acceptance of the Telecom Providers project product documented and distributed?

1123. Was the client satisfied with the Telecom Providers project results?

5.0 Closing Process Group: Telecom Providers

1124. Did you do what you said you were going to do?

1125. How dependent is the Telecom Providers project on other Telecom Providers projects or work efforts?

1126. When will the Telecom Providers project be done?

1127. How well did the team follow the chosen processes?

1128. Can the lesson learned be replicated?

1129. Are there funding or time constraints?

1130. What areas were overlooked on this Telecom Providers project?

1131. Were cost budgets met?

1132. What will you do?

1133. Did the Telecom Providers project team have the right skills?

1134. How well did the chosen processes produce the expected results?

1135. What was learned?

1136. Will the Telecom Providers project deliverable(s) replace a current asset or group of assets?

1137. What areas were overlooked on this Telecom Providers project?

1138. Is there a clear cause and effect between the activity and the lesson learned?

5.1 Procurement Audit: Telecom Providers

1139. Was the estimation of contract value in accordance with the criteria fixed in the Directive?

1140. Are there procedures for trade-in arrangements?

1141. In case of time and material and labour hour contracts, does surveillance give an adequate and reasonable assurance that the contractor is using efficient methods and effective cost controls?

1142. When competitive dialogue was used, did the contracting authority provide sufficient justification for the use of this procedure and was the contract actually particularly complex?

1143. Are the official minutes written in a clear and concise manner?

1144. Are obtained prices/qualities competitive to prices/qualities obtained by other procurement functions/units, comparing obtained or improved value for money?

1145. Does the procurement process compile basic procurement information such as how much is bought and spend with individual suppliers?

1146. Is a cost/benefit analysis, a cost/effectiveness or a financial analysis considering life-cycle costs performed and is the funding of the procurement guaranteed?

1147. Are there inferior competencies among procurement staff?

1148. Are advance payments to employees properly authorized and controlled?

1149. Who are the key suppliers?

1150. Has your organization fulfilled its obligations related to the payment of social security contributions and taxes?

1151. Is it tested periodically, whether your organizations way of handling tasks is competitive in relation to price and quality?

1152. Is the opportunity properly published?

1153. Is there time waste during tendering?

1154. Were all admitted tenderers invited to submit a tender for each specific contract?

1155. Are there mechanisms in place to evaluate the performance of the departments suppliers?

1156. Are all purchase orders reviewed by someone other than the individual preparing the purchase order (reasonableness of order and vendor selection)?

1157. Are employees with cash disbursement responsibilities required to take scheduled vacations?

1158. Were results of the award procedures published?

5.2 Contract Close-Out: Telecom Providers

1159. Have all contracts been closed?

1160. Change in circumstances?

1161. What happens to the recipient of services?

1162. Change in attitude or behavior?

1163. What is capture management?

1164. How/when used ?

1165. Have all acceptance criteria been met prior to final payment to contractors?

1166. Was the contract complete without requiring numerous changes and revisions?

1167. How does it work?

1168. Change in knowledge?

1169. Was the contract type appropriate?

1170. How is the contracting office notified of the automatic contract close-out?

1171. Parties: Authorized?

1172. Was the contract sufficiently clear so as not to

result in numerous disputes and misunderstandings?

1173. Has each contract been audited to verify acceptance and delivery?

1174. Parties: who is involved?

1175. Are the signers the authorized officials?

1176. Have all contracts been completed?

1177. Have all contract records been included in the Telecom Providers project archives?

5.3 Project or Phase Close-Out: Telecom Providers

1178. How often did each stakeholder need an update?

1179. What was expected from each stakeholder?

1180. Planned remaining costs?

1181. Who are the Telecom Providers project stakeholders and what are roles and involvement?

1182. Who exerted influence that has positively affected or negatively impacted the Telecom Providers project?

1183. What benefits or impacts does the stakeholder group expect to obtain as a result of the Telecom Providers project?

1184. Planned completion date?

1185. What could be done to improve the process?

1186. What are the informational communication needs for each stakeholder?

1187. Was the schedule met?

1188. Were the outcomes different from the already stated planned?

1189. Is the lesson based on actual Telecom Providers project experience rather than on independent research?

1190. What were the goals and objectives of the communications strategy for the Telecom Providers project?

1191. What are the marketing communication needs for each stakeholder?

1192. When and how were information needs best met?

1193. What hierarchical authority does the stakeholder have in your organization?

1194. What could have been improved?

1195. What were the desired outcomes?

5.4 Lessons Learned: Telecom Providers

1196. How well were Telecom Providers project issues communicated throughout your involvement in the Telecom Providers project?

1197. How actively and meaningfully were stakeholders involved in the Telecom Providers project?

1198. How effective was Telecom Providers project Team member training?

1199. Will the information remain current?

1200. Is the lesson based on actual Telecom Providers project experience rather than on independent research?

1201. Is the lesson significant, valid, and applicable?

1202. Was there a Telecom Providers project Definition document. Was there a Telecom Providers project Plan. Were they used during the Telecom Providers project?

1203. How clearly defined were the objectives for this Telecom Providers project?

1204. How will you allocate your funding resources?

1205. What policy constraints are relevant?

1206. If issue escalation was required, how effectively were issues resolved?

1207. Why does your organization need a lessons learned (LL) capability?

1208. Do you have any real problems?

1209. How effective was the acceptance management process?

1210. What is the quality and content of communication?

1211. What are your lessons learned that you will keep in mind for the next Telecom Providers project you participate in?

1212. Who managed most of the communication within the Telecom Providers project?

1213. Does the lesson describe a function that would be done differently the next time?

1214. What is the proportion of in-house and contractor personnel authorized for the Telecom Providers project?

Index

problem   15-17, 19, 21, 25, 27-28, 31, 34, 36, 45, 49, 60, 63,
168, 216, 219, 222, 244
problems   17, 19, 22, 24, 75, 77-78, 94, 102, 132-133, 141,
186, 196, 261
procedure   245-246, 253
procedures   9, 83, 96-99, 147, 151-152, 163, 168, 176, 182, 186,
193, 222, 229, 241, 253, 255
proceed   152
proceeding   170, 206
process   1-7, 9, 28, 31, 35-38, 41-42, 45, 57, 59-60, 62-65,
67-72, 75, 86, 89-92, 94-96, 99, 126, 128-129, 133-134, 137, 139-
141, 143, 146-148, 163, 167, 175, 186-187, 196-197, 207-208, 211,
214, 219, 223, 227-229, 232, 234, 237, 243, 247, 250-251, 253, 258,
261
processes   47, 58, 62-65, 67-68, 71, 89, 92, 95, 126-127, 133,
145, 147-148, 168, 175, 182, 187, 221, 229, 237, 251
produce   58, 133, 163, 216, 251
produced   61, 79, 238
produces   157
producing   143, 146
product   1, 59, 69, 101, 116, 129, 139, 146, 148, 159, 173,
180-182, 185, 196, 198, 210, 216-217, 227-228, 243, 245, 250
production   40, 86, 102, 148, 229
products   1, 18, 20, 55, 114, 129, 134, 143, 200, 214, 217,
221, 238, 240, 245
profession   197
profits 181
program   16, 48, 66, 98, 127, 129, 134, 182, 199, 233, 237-
238, 246
programme   238
programs   216, 236
progress   32, 43, 74, 97, 122, 128, 138, 148, 153, 178, 187,
231, 238
project2-8, 19, 22, 24, 31, 51, 61, 66, 68, 85, 91, 93, 104-107, 109,
114, 117, 120-122, 125-138, 140-143, 145-158, 161-162, 165-168,
170-178, 180-181, 183, 188-194, 196-203, 206-207, 210-211, 214-
217, 220, 227-228, 237, 239, 243-244, 247, 249-252, 257-261
projected   188, 242
projects   2, 52, 110, 118, 125-127, 143, 149, 153, 167-168,
174, 180, 190, 198, 201, 216-217, 230, 236, 243-244, 251
promising   116
promote   55, 68
promotions   137, 224

CPSIA information can be obtained
at www.ICGtesting.com
Printed in the USA
BVHW041011200819
556236BV00011B/736/P